4th Workshop on Events: Definition, Detection, Coreference, and Representation 2016

Held at the 2016 Conference of the North American Chapter of the Association for Computational Linguistics: Human Language Technologies (NAACL HLT 2016)

San Diego, California, USA
17 June 2016

ISBN: 978-1-5108-2520-8

Printed from e-media with permission by:

Curran Associates, Inc.
57 Morehouse Lane
Red Hook, NY 12571

Some format issues inherent in the e-media version may also appear in this print version.

Printed by Curran Associates, Inc. (2016)

For permission requests, please contact the Association for Computational Linguistics at the address below.

Association for Computational Linguistics
209 N. Eighth Street
Stroudsburg, Pennsylvania 18360

Phone: 1-570-476-8006
Fax: 1-570-476-0860

acl@aclweb.org

Additional copies of this publication are available from:

Curran Associates, Inc.
57 Morehouse Lane
Red Hook, NY 12571 USA
Phone: 845-758-0400
Fax: 845-758-2634
Email: curran@proceedings.com
Web: www.proceedings.com

NAACL HLT 2016

The 4th Workshop on Events: Definition, Detection, Coreference, and Representation

Proceedings of the Workshop

June 17, 2016
San Diego, California, USA

The Fourth Events Workshop

The **Events Workshop** is devoted to bringing together scholars interested in the definition, representation, and detection of events, event coreference, and relationships between events. After previous successful workshops co-located with NAACL 2013, ACL 2014, and NAACL 2015, the 4th Events workshop will take place on June 17 in San Diego and is co-located with NAACL-HLT 2016. We hope that this workshop will continue the tradition of having discussion-oriented workshop focused on bringing together different perspectives on these issues.

Event definition and detection has a number of large divisions, largely due to differences in which events are annotated. Many annotations only consider events within a particular domain or ontology, as in LDC's ACE and Machine Reading event annotation, or define other conditions (such as only looking at realis events). We hope to foster conversation between those dealing with "all events" approaches (where event detection has approached human performance in the recent Clinical Tempeval evaluations (Bethard et al. 2015)) and those dealing with added constraints added by specific ontologies or domains.

Dramatic strides also have been taken in event coreference. Event coreference has been driven by the event coreference annotations of ACE and Ontonotes, and the cross-document annotations of the ECB (Bejan and Harabagiu (2010, extended by Lee et al. (2012) and Cybulska and Vossen (2014)), but large questions remain, particularly with regard to how complicated phenomena related to coreference should be treated, such as bridging anaphora and subevent relationships between events (Poesio and Artstein 2005; 2008, Recasens et al. 2011, Hovy et al. 2013, Araki et al. 2014), and with regard to methodologies for developing large, high-quality corpora of event coreference.

Similarly, the relationships between events (as with temporal or causal relations), and the relationships between events and larger structures (such as scripts, timelines, or larger events) are important factors in event understanding. TimeML (Pustejovsky, et. al., 2010), or temporal relation annotation, has held numerous Semeval tasks regarding detection of temporal relations. Other relations between events, such as causation (Bethard and Martin 2008; Mizra et al. 2014) or contradiction detection (De Marneffe et al. 2008), have been studied. Building consensus regarding how relations such as causation should be represented, annotated and detection is an ongoing frontier or research.

The seven papers accepted for the workshop illustrate this wide range of work now being done on events. The papers cover a range of topics; from proposals of new tasks and corpora detecting highly relevant events, to proposed annotations of internal representation of event aspect or event-related features, to annotation of causal and temporal relations between events, to works introducing, analyzing, or discussing the evaluation of event and event coreference corpora. This workshop continues the format of previous Events workshops by having a poster session to showcase these projects from around the world.

This iteration of the workshop will have a focus on discussions between different approaches to events. We are honored to have the participation of multiple eminent speakers who can represent those different approaches: Dan Roth, Eduard Hovy, Collin Baker, Sergei Nirenburg and Marjorie McShane.

Organizers:

Martha Palmer, University of Colorado Boulder
Tim O'Gorman, University of Colorado Boulder
Teruko Mitamura, Carnegie Mellon University
Eduard Hovy, Carnegie Mellon University

Invited Speakers:

Dan Roth, University of Illinois Urbana-Champaign
Collin Baker, University of California Berkeley
Sergei Nirenburg, Rensselaer Polytechnic Institute
Marjorie McShane, Rensselaer Polytechnic Institute
Eduard Hovy, Carnegie Mellon University

Program Committee:

Dan Bikel, LinkedIn, Inc
Rodolfo Delmonte, Universitá Ca' Foscari
Robert Frederking, Carnegie Mellon University
Marjorie Freedman, BBN Technologies
Boyan Onyshkevych, Department of Defense
James Pustejovsky, Brandeis University
Marta Recasens, Google Inc.
Tomohide Shibata, Kyoto University
Ian Soboroff, NIST
Stephanie Strassel, Linguistic Data Consortium
Mihai Surdeanu, University of Arizona
Lucy Vanderwende, Microsoft
Piek Vossen, VU University Amsterdam
Luke Zettlemoyer, University of Washington
Alexis Palmer, Heidelberg University
Annemarie Friedrich, Universitat des Saarlandes
Bernardo Magnini, Fondazione Bruno Kessler
Sara Tonelli, Fondazione Bruno Kessler
German Rigau, Universidad del Pais Vasco
Steven Bethard, University of Alabama at Birmingham
Nate Chambers, United States Naval Academy
Travis Wolfe, John Hopkins University
Rachel Rudinger, John Hopkins University
Ann Bies, Linguistic Data Consortium

Table of Contents

This page intentionally left blank.

Conference Program

Friday, June 17, 2016

9:00–10:30 ***Events and Ontologies: A debate between Collin Baker, Sergei Nirenburg and Marjorie McShane***

11:00–12:30 ***Trusting human or automated analysis: A debate between Dan Roth and Eduard Hovy***

1:00–2:30 ***Poster Session***

"Making the News": Identifying Noteworthy Events in News Articles
Shyam Upadhyay, Christos Christodoulopoulos and Dan Roth

Annotation of causal and aspectual structure of events in RED: a preliminary report
William Croft, Pavlina Peskova and Michael Regan

Multimodal Use of an Upper-Level Event Ontology
Claire Bonial, David Tahmoush, Susan Windisch Brown and Martha Palmer

A Comparison of Event Representations in DEFT
Ann Bies, Zhiyi Song, Jeremy Getman, Joe Ellis, Justin Mott, Stephanie Strassel, Martha Palmer, Teruko Mitamura, Marjorie Freedman, Heng Ji and Tim O'Gorman

Event Nugget and Event Coreference Annotation
Zhiyi Song, Ann Bies, Stephanie Strassel, Joe Ellis, Teruko Mitamura, Hoa Trang Dang, Yukari Yamakawa and Sue Holm

Constructing a Dictionary Describing Feature Changes of Arguments in Event Sentences
Tetsuaki Nakamura and Daisuke Kawahara

CaTeRS: Causal and Temporal Relation Scheme for Semantic Annotation of Event Structures
Nasrin Mostafazadeh, Alyson Grealish, Nathanael Chambers, James Allen and Lucy Vanderwende

2:30–3:30 ***Comparison of event annotations on shared task (discussion led by Martha Palmer)***

4:00–5:00 ***Event Sequencing, Annotation and Evaluation (discussion led by Teruko Mitamura)***

"Making the News": Identifying Noteworthy Events in News Articles

Shyam Upadhyay and **Christos Christodoulopoulos** and **Dan Roth**
Department of Computer Science
University of Illinois at Urbana-Champaign
{upadhya3,christod,danr}@illinois.edu

Abstract

Most events described in a news article are background events – only a small number are noteworthy, and a even smaller number serve as the trigger for writing of that article. Although these events are difficult to identify, they are crucial to NLP tasks such as first story detection, document summarization and event coreference, and to many applications of event analysis that depend on event counting and identifying trends. In this work, we introduce the notion of *news-peg*, a concept borrowed from the political science literature, in an attempt to remedy this problem. A news-peg is an event which prompted the author to write the article, and it serves as a more fine-grained measure of noteworthiness than a summary. We describe a new task of news-peg identification and release an annotated dataset for its evaluation. We formalize an operational definition of a news-peg, on which human annotators achieve high inter-annotator agreement (over 80%), and present a rule-based system for this task, which exploits syntactic features derived from established journalistic devices.

1 Introduction

The narratives in news articles often follow certain established styles, such as *inverted pyramid* reporting, to emphasize certain parts more than others. Such narratives nicely illustrate discourse level texture – parts which supply the main points and are crucial to conveying information constitute the *foreground*, while the parts which assist in providing supporting facts or setting the scene are referred to as *background* (Hopper and Thompson, 1980).

> Grigory Pasko, crusading Russian journalist who documented Russian Navy's mishandling of nuclear waste, is **released** on parole after serving two-thirds of his four-year prison sentence.

Figure 1: A human-generated summary from the New York Times Corpus with event predicates and the news-peg shown underlined and in **bold** respectively.

When reasoning about events in news articles, such document level texture necessitates the ability to distinguish foreground objects from background. Event recognition alone is not sufficient to make such distinctions, and the roles these events play in framing of a given story. Consider the summary shown in Figure 1 – it is easy to infer that the "release" event is the reason why the news article was written, and other events are present merely to qualify the entities present. Distinguishing the "release" event from others can help understanding what the document is reporting.

This paper introduces *news-peg identification*: a new task aimed at finding events which triggered the creation of the news article. Our notion of news-peg serves (formally defined in §4) as a measure of noteworthiness, assessing how much was the event responsible in prompting the author to write the article. Such events are also called dominant news elements in the social science literature. Note that news-pegs determine a stronger measure of noteworthiness than summaries, as a summary can contain events which are not news-pegs. We discuss how the ability to identify news-pegs can aid progress in several NLP tasks.

The contributions of our work are as follows:

Proceedings of the 4th Workshop on Events: Definition, Detection, Coreference, and Representation, pages 1–7,
San Diego, California, June 17, 2016.

- We define a new task, news-peg identification, and annotate data for its evaluation.
- We experimentally demonstrate the feasibility of the task, by showing a high inter-annotator agreement of 81.3% on a manually annotated evaluation dataset of 100 documents.
- We also evaluate several baseline approaches which exploit syntax to identify news-pegs and propose a rule-based approach which attains a F1 score of 54.7 points.

2 Motivation

The knowledge of whether an event is a news-peg in a news article can prove useful for several tasks. We briefly describe a few application below:

Cross-Document Event Coreference The notion of a news-peg is closely related to that of a non-anaphoric entities in the task of *entity coreference*; instead of looking for intra-document event mentions however, we look across documents. During the lifetime of an event, it is a news-peg for a short duration near its origin, as it is likely that several news sources deem it newsworthy at that time. Therefore, if an event is a news-peg, it is unlikely that it will refer to an earlier event instance (in a different article). It has been shown that detecting whether an entity is non-anaphoric benefits entity-level coreference resolution (Peng et al., 2015; de Marneffe et al., 2015; Wiseman et al., 2015; Ng, 2004; Ng and Cardie, 2002) – we expect cross-document event coreference to benefit in a similar way from news-peg identification.

First Story Detection (FSD) Current approaches to FSD (Petrović et al., 2010; Petrović et al., 2012) use similarity metrics like Latent Semantic Hashing (Salakhutdinov and Hinton, 2009) and use an inverted index to compare it with $O(1)$ ($\approx$ 1000) of the most recent documents. A shortcoming of this problem formulation is that they treat the entire document as a event and do not account for multiple events in the same document. This formulation works well with tweets (assuming most tweets describe a single event) but is unsatisfactory when working with news articles. If we allow for n events in a document (on average), the number of comparisons will be $O(n^2)$.

A news-peg, on the other hand, identifies the reported event and thus allows us to focus on the most noteworthy event in the article, bringing the number of comparisons back to $O(1)$. Using news-pegs we can also perform a heuristic pruning of this search space, by allowing the system to ignore documents which do not have a similar event as their news-peg. For instance, if a newly arrived article describes a bombing event, we can prune out all articles from the 1000 most recent articles whose news-peg was not a bombing event.

Event Linking Nothman et al. (2012) introduced event linking as the task of grounding a event mention (*referent*) to a article in a news archive that first reports it (*anchor article*). They noted that annotating a large corpus was impractical because of the under-specification of "newsworthiness" and because the same article can be the anchor for some events and not for others. Annotation effort can be significantly reduced by knowing what is being reported for the first time in a document as it narrows the set of possible events the document can be an anchor for. News-pegs can help in segmenting a document into events which are being reported for the first time, and events which convey background information.

Document Summarization Even though we propose to use summarization as a sub-routine in our system (§5), a good news-peg classifier can prove useful to a summarization system. Any good summary for a document must contain a reference to its news-peg, as it is the most noteworthy among all events in the document. Drawing on this intuition, we can use the presence/absence of a news-peg as a alternative measure of quality of a summarization. Moreover, extractive summarization (Carbonell and Goldstein, 1998) approaches can prune out sentences which do not contain (or refer to) the news-peg, thereby reducing the search space of sentences from which the summary is constructed.

NLP applications such as Event Timeline Construction (Do et al., 2012) and headline generation (Woodsend and Lapata, 2012; Alfonseca et al., 2013) can benefit similarly from news-pegs.

3 Related Work

Attempts to distinguish foreground and background regions in text date back to the 1980s. Decker (1985) generated summaries from newspaper reports, where they used deterministic syntactic rules to label foreground events. These rules were based on predictable reporting styles in journalism such as the *inverted pyramid* and *block paragraph*[1], and drew heavily on the syntactic correlation between grounding and information content. We analyze the performance of these rules for news-peg identification in our experiments (§6).

The study of dominant elements of discourse has been formally studied in linguistics as a part of *centering theory* (Grosz et al., 1995), a broader theory of attention and coherence in discourse, both of which were analyzed on a document-level basis (i.e. local discourse). The authors suggested the use of centering constructs to keep track of the key entities, which change with discourse.

Document-level importance of entities (which include events) was explored by Gamon et al. (2013). The authors use the term *salience* to denote entity importance and graded entities into 3 categories – most salient, less salient, not salient. They extracted supervision from web-search logs to semi-automatically obtain noisy salience judgments for a large web corpus. Salient entities in a web document were then identified using graph centrality measures.

Our event extraction approach (§4.1) closely resembles the Open-IE event extraction approach (Fader et al., 2011; Hu et al., 2013; Do et al., 2011) which views events as sentence-level relations. Events are extracted via syntactic and lexical constraints, which are imposed on sentence level structure, such as dependency parse. For example, Sun et al. (2015) use the *nsubj* and *dobj* relations to identify relation pairs, which are then merged if they share the same predicate to form a `(Subj,Pred,Obj)` tuple expressing an event. Unlike traditional event paradigms like ACE (NIST, 2004) and ERE (ERE, 2013), the Open-IE event paradigm enjoys portability and domain-independence.

[1] Also known as *nut-paragraph*.

4 News-Peg Definition

In this section we define what constitutes an event and then formally describe the criteria to determine if an event is a news-peg. We use the example sentences marked with events and news-pegs in Table 1 to help us illustrate our definition.

4.1 Event Extraction

Definition 1 *An event is a predicate-argument structure, whose predicate (verbal or nominal) describes a single occurrence (eg. died, married) or an aggregate of occurrences (eg. elections, shootings etc.).*

We adopt a event extraction approach based on FrameNet (Baker et al., 1998). We automatically generate a set of *acceptable frames* from FrameNet which are associated with events of our interest. This list dictates the frames of the occurrences that we will consider events. For each predicate-argument structure, we identify the frame evoked by the predicate, and accept it as an event if the triggered frame belongs to the set of acceptable frames.

4.2 News-Peg Definition

Team of French archaeologists **work** at piece-by-piece reconstruction of ancient Baphuon temple in Siem Reap, Cambodia.
Kuwait's Interior Ministry says young Kuwaiti man who fled to Saudi Arabia after terrorist shooting in Kuwait that killed one American and wounded another has **confessed** to the attack.
Three Israeli soldiers are **shot** and **killed** in what Israeli officials describe as **ambush** by Palestinian gunmen near West Bank city of Hebron.
Bush administration officials have **concluded** that international inspectors are unlikely to find tangible and irrefutable evidence that Iraq is hiding weapons of mass destruction so administration is **preparing** its own assessment that will rely heavily on evidence from Iraqi defectors.
United Nations Security Council took grueling nine weeks to **negotiate** Nov. 8 resolution to make Iraq give up its illegal weapons, and now United States may have to go courting again to secure votes of five countries that have just become non-permanent members.

Table 1: Example sentences where event predicates identified by our extraction approach are underlined, and news-peg predicates appear in bold.

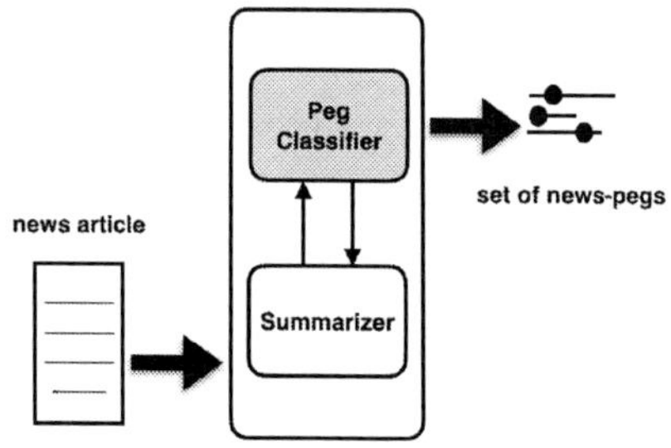

Figure 2: Schematic diagram of an end-to-end system. We evaluate the news-peg classifier (gray box), controlling for other sources of error by using a human generated summary. It is possible that the summarizer and news-peg classifier operate jointly.

Definition 2 *An event is a news-peg for an article if it was responsible in prompting the author to write the article.*

Two (or more) event predicates can be news-pegs if they are being co-reported (both are stated as if reported for the first time). For example, in Table 1, the third and fourth examples have events being co-reported (*shoot*, *kill* and *ambush* are co-reported, similarly concluded and preparing are co-reported). We allow a document to have multiple news-pegs, provided neither one of them heads a predicate which takes the other as an argument. For example, in Table 1, in the second example, the *fled*, *shooting* and *killed* events all are mentioned only to qualify the entity, and serve as elaboration for the news-peg, the *confessed* event. This ensures that events which appear under elaborative or subordinating clauses are not marked as news-pegs.

Reporting of events in news articles is often made indirectly by using journalistic devices such as *hedging* (example 2 in Table 1). Other complications arise from light verb constructions, such as the phrase "took grueling nine weeks to negotiate" in example 5 of Table 1. To mitigate this, we demand that the marked news-peg is not indirectly reporting another potentially more noteworthy news-peg. In case of light verb constructs, we consider the noun in the construct as the news-peg. So the news-peg in "took grueling nine weeks to negotiate" is "negotiate" instead of "took".

Note that our definition operates under the assumption that whether a event is an news-peg can be determined using document local discourse alone, without appealing to cross-document discourse. This assumption resonates with the local scoping assumption made by Gamon et al. (2013).

5 News-Peg Identification

We describe the task of identifying news-pegs as follows,

Input: A piece of text (news article/summary of a news article).

Output: A set of events in that piece of text that are the news-pegs.

Note that we intentionally do not specify if the piece of text is a document or a summary, because a document could have multiple news-pegs (albeit referents of the same event), which introduces the issue of event coreference (NIST, 2004). Ideally, the output would contain a cluster of events all of which refer to a news-peg. A possible strategy to circumvent this problem would be to first generate a summary (or the k-best summaries) and then obtain news-peg judgements per summary. Figure 2 shows a diagram for such an end-to-end system, where a news document is first summarized before identifying the news-peg.

When evaluating a news-peg classifier, using system-generated summaries would be unfair as we cannot judge whether the classifier or the summarizer is the source of error. To prevent this, we annotated the human generated summaries of the sampled documents, and ran the news-peg classifier on these summaries. While this is not the appropriate evaluation for an end-to-end system which would accept documents as input, we want to analyze the performance of the news-peg identification subroutine, for which summary level analysis suffices. Using the summary also precludes the need for event coreference.

5.1 Baselines

We use deterministic syntactic rules as baselines. To generate these features, we use the pipeline described in §6. We evaluate the following baseline approaches.

- **Active Voice**: If the event predicate appears in the active voice, mark it as the news-peg.
- **Main Clause**: If the event predicate appears in a main clause, mark it as the news-peg.

Algorithm 1 Rule-Based Classifier

```
Input: Event Predicate P
Output: Label L whether the predicate is a news-peg
if Voice(P) = Active OR Clause(P) = Main then
    L ← 1
end if
if Clause(P) = Relative then
    L ← 0
end if
if Type(P) = Verb AND !Appositive(P) AND
  !FirstNonAppositiveVerbal(P) then
    L ← 0
end if
return L
```

- **First Predicate**: If the event predicate is the first predicate of the first sentence, mark it as the news-peg.

5.2 Rule-Based Classifier

We also developed a rule based system, shown in Algorithm 1, which uses a combination of these syntactic constructs used in the baselines to identify news-pegs. The classifier can be viewed as a decision list which deterministically predicts the label for a predicate. The primitives `Appositive`(P) detects if the predicate is embedded inside an appositive, while the primitive `FirstNonAppositiveVerbal`(P) returns true if the predicate is the first such verbal predicate which is not inside an appositive.

6 Experimental Analysis

We use the New York Times Annotated Corpus (Sandhaus, 2008) for all our experiments. The corpus contains around 650k documents annotated with human-generated summaries. We only work with the "World News" section of the corpus from 2003 to 2007. We randomly sampled 100 articles to be manually annotated and used for evaluation.

We generated the list of acceptable frames by identifying the frame evoked by each event trigger in ACE (NIST, 2004) and ERE (ERE, 2013). We use this list of frames to determine whether a predicate-argument structure qualifies as an event. For identifying the frame evoked by a given predicate, we use the state-of-the-art frame-identifier packaged in SEMAFOR (Das and Smith, 2011). For our event extraction, all the documents were annotated using Illinois-SRL (Punyakanok et al., 2008), a state-of-the-art SRL system, to identify nominal and verbal predicates. Note that we do not take into account semantic role assignments, as we believe this does not have any consequence on event extraction.

To extract features, we use the constituency and dependency parser from Stanford CoreNLP (Manning et al., 2014) to identify the clause structure of sentences. Any clause labeled "SBAR" is considered subordinate, and a subordinate clause starting with a *Wh-* word is considered relative[2]. All remaining clauses are considered main. To identify appositions, we used the Illinois-Comma-SRL (Arivazhagan et al., 2016) package.

6.1 Annotation Setup

We obtained news-peg judgments using the Brat annotation tool (Stenetorp et al., 2012) from two annotators[3]. Each annotator was shown the human generated summary from New York Times Corpus, where event predicates detected by our event extraction procedure (§4.1) were highlighted. They were prompted with the definition of a news-peg from §4.2 and were instructed to mark the predicate(s) which they believed to indicate the news-peg(s). In case the news-peg was not one of the extracted events, the annotators were instructed to mark it.

Inter-annotator agreement was computed on how often the annotators mark the same predicate as the news-peg. The annotators achieved a high agreement of 81.3% on the 100 documents[4]. The judgments were then adjudicated by the first author. Out of 699 event predicates identified in the sampled 100 document summaries, only 103 were identified as news-pegs, accounting for only 14% of all verbal and nominal predicates.

6.2 Results

Table 2 shows the performance of the baselines and the rule based classifier on the manually annotated test data. The best performing system is the rule-

[2] *Wh*-words are what, who, whom, that, which, where, whose, whether

[3] Not the authors.

[4] We counted agreement only if annotators agreed on all news-peg predicate(s) in a document.

Approach	P	R	F1
Active Voice	31.0	54.3	39.4
Main Clause	22.2	**62.1**	32.7
First Predicate	41.0	37.9	39.4
Rule-Based Classifier	**68.1**	45.6	**54.7**

Table 2: Results comparing baselines and the rule based classifier. The classifier outperforms the baselines, but still achieves moderate F1 scores.

Three recent defectors from North Korea living in South Korea draw on their experience to **give** their own proposals for how to deal with unpredictable government of their impoverished homeland.
United Nations weapons inspectors in Iraq make dramatic use of their authority, **closing** exits and entrances to any site where they are working and **confining** thousands of people at sprawling government research complex, including Iraqi ambassador to UN, for almost six hours.

Table 3: Some hard examples from our test dataset where none of the compared approaches identified the correct news-peg (shown in **bold**).

based classifier, which is still far from human performance in terms of accuracy. It is evident that there is a lot of room for improvement.

A few examples that the rule-based classifier got wrong are shown in Table 3. The examples show that use of elaboration (eg. "draw on their experience") and light verb construction (eg. "make [...] use of authority") complicates the task. In the first example, the action being reported is the transfer of information from the defectors and what the information is about is auxilary information (therefore "deal" is not the news-peg). We believe that more discourse-aware features will be needed to improve performance.

7 Conclusion and Future Directions

In this paper, we proposed the new task of news-peg identification, and formalized a definition of news-pegs and shown its feasibility. We listed a number of applications which can benefit from a news-peg classifier. We also developed a rule-based news-peg classifier, which can be good basis for future work.

We also proposed an end-to-end system which relies on the synergy of a summarizer and news-peg classifier for identifying news-pegs. In future work, we plan to investigate if jointly training a summarizer and a news-peg can actually improve performance of both systems. Also, the availability of human summaries from the New York Times Corpus opens the possibilities of exploring semi-supervised training approaches for news-peg classification.

Acknowledgments

We would like to thank Joel Nothman, Dan Shalmon, Scott Althaus, and the anonymous reviewers for their valuable suggestions and guidance. This work was supported by Contract HR0011-15-2-0025 with the US Defense Advanced Research Projects Agency (DARPA) and DARPA agreement number FA8750-13-2-0008. Approved for Public Release, Distribution Unlimited. The views expressed are those of the authors and do not reflect the official policy or position of the Department of Defense or the U.S. Government.

References

Enrique Alfonseca, Daniele Pighin, and Guillermo Garrido. 2013. Heady: News headline abstraction through event pattern clustering. In *Proceedings of the 51st Annual Meeting of the ACL*, pages 1243–1253. Association for Computational Linguistics.

Naveen Arivazhagan, Christos Christodoulopoulos, and Dan Roth. 2016. Labeling the semantic roles of commas. In *AAAI*.

Collin F. Baker, Charles J. Fillmore, and John B. Lowe. 1998. The Berkeley FrameNet project. In *Proceedings of the 36th Annual Meeting of the ACL and 17th International Conference on Computational Linguistics - Volume 1*, ACL '98, pages 86–90, Stroudsburg, PA, USA. Association for Computational Linguistics.

Jaime Carbonell and Jade Goldstein. 1998. The use of MMR, diversity-based reranking for reordering documents and producing summaries. SIGIR '98, pages 335–336, New York, NY, USA. ACM.

Dipanjan Das and Noah A Smith. 2011. Semi-supervised frame-semantic parsing for unknown predicates. In *Proceedings of the 49th Annual Meeting of the ACL-HLT*, pages 1435–1444. Association for Computational Linguistics.

Marie-Catherine de Marneffe, Marta Recasens, and Christopher Potts. 2015. Modeling the lifespan of discourse entities with application to coreference resolution. *JAIR*, 52:445–475.

Nan Decker. 1985. The use of syntactic clues in discourse processing. In *Proceedings of the 23rd annual meeting on ACL*, pages 315–323. Association for Computational Linguistics.

Quang Xuan Do, Yee Seng Chan, and Dan Roth. 2011. Minimally supervised event causality identification. In *Proceedings of the Conference on EMNLP*, pages 294–303. Association for Computational Linguistics.

Quang Xuan Do, Wei Lu, and Dan Roth. 2012. Joint inference for event timeline construction. In *EMNLP*.

2013. Linguistic data consortium, DEFT ERE annotation guidelines: Events v1.1.

Anthony Fader, Stephen Soderland, and Oren Etzioni. 2011. Identifying relations for open information extraction. In *Proceedings of the Conference on EMNLP*, pages 1535–1545. Association for Computational Linguistics.

Michael Gamon, Tae Yano, Xinying Song, Johnson Apacible, and Patrick Pantel. 2013. Identifying salient entities in web pages. In *Proceedings of the 22nd ACM international conference on Conference on information & knowledge management*, pages 2375–2380. ACM.

Barbara J. Grosz, Scott Weinstein, and Aravind K. Joshi. 1995. Centering: A framework for modeling the local coherence of discourse. *Comput. Linguist.*, 21(2):203–225, June.

Paul Hopper and Sandra A. Thompson. 1980. Transitivity in grammar and discourse. *Language*, 56:251–299.

Zhichao Hu, Elahe Rahimtoroghi, Larissa Munishkina, Reid Swanson, and A. Marilyn Walker. 2013. Unsupervised induction of contingent event pairs from film scenes. In *Proceedings of the 2013 Conference on EMNLP*, pages 369–379. Association for Computational Linguistics.

Christopher D. Manning, Mihai Surdeanu, John Bauer, Jenny Finkel, Steven J. Bethard, and David McClosky. 2014. The Stanford CoreNLP natural language processing toolkit. In *Proceedings of 52nd Annual Meeting of the ACL: System Demonstrations*, pages 55–60.

Vincent Ng and Claire Cardie. 2002. Identifying anaphoric and non-anaphoric noun phrases to improve coreference resolution. In *COLING 2002: The 19th International Conference on Computational Linguistics*.

Vincent Ng. 2004. Learning noun phrase anaphoricity to improve conference resolution: Issues in representation and optimization. In *Proceedings of the 42nd Annual Meeting of the ACL*.

NIST. 2004. The ACE evaluation plan.

Joel Nothman, Matthew Honnibal, Ben Hachey, and James R Curran. 2012. Event linking: Grounding event reference in a news archive. In *Proceedings of the 50th Annual Meeting of the ACL: Short Papers-Volume 2*, pages 228–232. Association for Computational Linguistics.

Haoruo Peng, Kai-Wei Chang, and Dan Roth. 2015. A joint framework for coreference resolution and mention head detection. In *CoNLL*, page 10, University of Illinois, Urbana-Champaign, Urbana, IL, 61801, 7. ACL.

Saša Petrović, Miles Osborne, and Victor Lavrenko. 2010. Streaming first story detection with application to twitter. In *The 2010 Annual Conference of the NAACL-HLT*, pages 181–189. Association for Computational Linguistics.

Saša Petrović, Miles Osborne, and Victor Lavrenko. 2012. Using paraphrases for improving first story detection in news and twitter. In *Proceedings of the 2012 Conference of the NAACL-HLT*, pages 338–346. Association for Computational Linguistics.

Vasin Punyakanok, Dan Roth, and Wen tau Yih. 2008. The importance of syntactic parsing and inference in semantic role labeling. *Computational Linguistics*, 34(2).

Ruslan Salakhutdinov and Geoffrey Hinton. 2009. Semantic hashing. *International Journal on Approximate Reasoning*, 50(7):969–978, July.

E. Sandhaus. 2008. The New York Times Annotated Corpus. *Linguistic Data Consortium, Philadelphia*, 6(12).

Pontus Stenetorp, Sampo Pyysalo, Goran Topić, Tomoko Ohta, Sophia Ananiadou, and Jun'ichi Tsujii. 2012. Brat: A web-based tool for nlp-assisted text annotation. In *Proceedings of the Demonstrations at the 13th Conference of the EACL*, pages 102–107, Avignon, France, April. Association for Computational Linguistics.

Rui Sun, Yue Zhang, Meishan Zhang, and Dong-Hong Ji. 2015. Event-driven headline generation. In *Proceedings of the 53rd Annual Meeting of the ACL*, pages 462–472. Association for Computational Linguistics.

Sam Wiseman, M. Alexander Rush, Stuart Shieber, and Jason Weston. 2015. Learning anaphoricity and antecedent ranking features for coreference resolution. In *Proceedings of the 53rd Annual Meeting of the ACL*, pages 1416–1426. Association for Computational Linguistics.

Kristian Woodsend and Mirella Lapata. 2012. Multiple aspect summarization using integer linear programming. In *Proceedings of the 2012 Joint Conference on EMNLP*, pages 233–243, Jeju Island, Korea, July. Association for Computational Linguistics.

Annotation of causal and aspectual structure of events in RED: a preliminary report

William Croft, Pavlina Pešková, Michael Regan
University of New Mexico
{wcroft,pavlinap,reganman}@unm.edu

Abstract

Causal and temporal relations among events are typically analyzed in terms of interclausal relations. Yet participants in a monoclausal event interact causally as well, and monoclausal events unfold in temporal phases. We propose an annotation scheme for the resulting analysis of event structure types. The annotation scheme is based on a fine-grained analysis of aspectual structure combined with a novel analysis of physical event types based on proposals in the theoretical linguistics literature. By decomposing complex events in a clause, we will ultimately model the overall dynamic causal network of entities interacting over time described in a text.

1 Introduction: Why annotate event decomposition?

Most analyses of event structure in text assume that a single clause headed by a verb denotes a single event; causal, temporal and other relations between events are assumed to hold between clauses. However, participants in a monoclausal event interact causally as well, and monoclausal events unfold in temporal phases. These observations underlie the decompositional analyses of verb meaning found widely in theoretical linguistics, both formal and cognitive, and used to capture linguistic generalizations. We use and extend the model of event decomposition of Croft (2012), intended to account for crosslinguistic generalizations, in order to develop an annotation scheme for event structure in single clauses.

A major issue in annotation of verb meaning is that a verb can be construed in multiple ways, largely though not entirely depending on the clausal constructions in which it occurs. For example, one and the same verb can describe events of different aspectual types (Moens and Steedman, 1988; Croft, 2012) (examples from COCA and Google Books):

(1) a. He **touched** the tip of his hat, then left a few bills on the bar and slid off his stool.
  b. But **touching** the wound again and again, and remaining concentrated on the wound is not going to heal it.
  c. We can say the chair is **touching** the wall it is leaning against, but there really is not an encounter between them, but only a spatial relation of contiguity.
  d. Her fingers **touched** the ball, and she gripped.
  e. The desert **touches** the boundaries of rural and urban settlements alike.

Example (1a) describes an instant of contact (usually called semelfactive); example (1b) an activity of repeated contact; example (1c) a transitory state of maintained contact; example (1d) an achievement (instantaneous change) from noncontact to contact, and example (1e) an inherent physical relationship between two landscape entities. The different aspectual interpretations are constrained partly by the tense-aspect construction (simple past, simple present, progressive) but also partly by contextual factors—for example, (1a) and (1d) are both simple past but have different aspectual interpretations.

Proceedings of the 4th Workshop on Events: Definition, Detection, Coreference, and Representation, pages 8–17,
San Diego, California, June 17, 2016.

The same ambiguity is found in the force-dynamic structure of events denoted by a single verb. Examples (2) and (3) illustrate the ambiguity, with the standard labels for the force-dynamic type given in brackets (examples from COCA and Google Books):

(2) a. Eva stayed by his side to hold the bowl, or to **wipe** his face with a cool cloth. [caused contact]

b. Remove from the heat and **wipe** the bottom of the bowl dry. [change of state]

c. Dad waved at us and stopped to **wipe** the sweat from his forehead. [removal]

d. He resisted the impulse to **wipe** them [hands] on his jeans. [application]

(3) a. She flailed with her feet to get her balance and managed to **kick** the chair. [contact]

b. So he's going to shoot if I have to **kick** him black and blue. [change of state]

c. **Kick** the ball into Lake Michigan... [ballistic motion]

d. Go on, **kick** him the ball and let's see what he'll do with it. [transfer]

e. You **kick** wildly at the plastic bottle, finally knocking it loose. [conative—action aimed towards a target entity]

In order to capture the aspectual and force-dynamic structure of an event necessary to build the dynamic causal network, a semantic analysis or semantic annotation of clauses in text will have to combine three elements: annotation of the verbal "root", the unanalyzed part of verb meaning (Levin and Rappaport Hovav, 2005); annotation of the aspectual type, or *aspectual image schema* as we will call it; and annotation of the *force-dynamic image schema*, corresponding roughly to the labels found in examples (2)–(3).

The goal of an annotation scheme is to allow annotators to identify semantic types and properties in a text with a degree of reliability to make the manually annotated corpus useful for training, and also to allow automated integration with formal reasoning (Mani and Pustejovsky, 2012). We therefore propose an annotation scheme with holistic labels for aspectual and causal event types. Force-dynamic and aspectual structure are annotated separately from verb meaning and from each other, because verb meaning does not determine aspectual or force-dynamic interpretation, as noted above. The aspectual and causal event types for a clause are the product of the combination of the verb meaning and the tense-aspect and argument structure constructions of the clause. The holistic annotation relieves the annotator of identifying the contribution of the construction vs. the predicate to the event's semantic structure. The aspectual and force dynamic annotations can be translated into the decompositional analyses described in this paper, which can in turn form the basis of formal reasoning about the events in a text.

The aspect and force-dynamic annotation scheme proposed here is intended to be included in Richer Event Description (RED), which in its current form primarily annotates time, modality, and event coreference (Ikuta et al., 2014). RED is being revamped to supplement the Abstract Meaning Representation (AMR) annotation schema (Banarescu et al., 2013). AMR uses PropBank framesets (Palmer et al., 2005) for verb meanings (the verbal "root"), annotating argument roles by numbers (arg0, arg1, etc.) instead of semantic role labels, as found in VerbNet (Kipper et al., 2007) or FrameNet (Fillmore et al., 2003). The aspect and force-dynamic annotations provide the event structure from which the semantic roles of the numbered arguments can be derived. The derivation of semantic roles from argument positions in an event decomposition has been argued for by many theoretical linguists (Croft, 1991; Dowty, 1991; Van Valin and LaPolla, 1997).

In addition, other relevant semantic inferences about the events in the text may be derived from the aspectual and force-dynamic decompositional event structures. We expect that automated post-processing of syntactically parsed, semantically annotated text will provide data for statistical analysis of the semantic interaction of constructions and verbs (more generally, complex predicates) in producing the event structure interpretation of a clause.

Event Types	Definition	Example	Other Terms/References
States			
Transitory	May change over an individual's lifetime	*He is sick.*	*stage-level predicates* (Carlson, 1979)
Inherent Permanent	Holds over an individual's lifetime	*She is French.*	*object-level predicates* (Carlson, 1979)
Acquired Permanent	Once acquired does not change	*This window is broken.*	
Point	Holds for one point in time	*The sun is at its zenith.*	(Mittwoch, 1988)
Achievements			
Reversible Directed	Ends in a transitory state	*The door opened.*	*resettable verbs* (Talmy, 1985)
Irreversible Directed	Ends in a permanent state	*The window broke.*	*nonresettable verbs* (Talmy, 1985)
Cyclic	Ends in a point state; reverts to the original state immediately afterwards	*The mouse squeaked.*	*semelfactives* (Smith, 1991), *point events* (Jackendoff, 1991), *full-cycle predicates* (Talmy, 1985)
Activities			
Directed	Describes an incremental change in a single direction on a scale	*The soup cooled.*	*degree achievements* (Dowty, 1979), *gradient verbs* (Talmy, 1985), *gradual completion verbs* (Bertinetto and Squartini, 1995)
Undirected	Describes change that is not incremental over time	*The girls chanted.*	*activities* (Vendler, 1957)
Accomplishments			
Incremental	Consists of a directed activity leading up to the defined result state	*I read the book.*	*accomplishments* (Vendler, 1957)
Nonincremental	Consists of an undirected activity leading up to the defined result state	*I repaired the computer.*	*progressive achievements* (Rothstein, 2004), *runup achievements* (Croft, 1998)

Table 1: Aspectual image schemas

2 Annotation of aspectual structure of events

Our annotation of aspect is considerably more fine-grained than previous annotations (Friedrich and Palmer, 2014; Mathew and Katz, 2009; Siegel and McKeown, 2001; Xue and Zhang, 2014; Zarcone and Lenci, 2008). It has long been known that the four-way aspectual classification of events by Vendler (1957) into states (static), activities (dynamic, durative, unbounded), achievements (dynamic, punctual, bounded) and accomplishments (dynamic, durative, bounded) does not appear to include a number of other aspectual types that have been described in the linguistics literature. Croft (2012) argues that all of the aspectual types that have been reported can be classified as different subtypes of Vendler's four classes. Table 1 summarizes Croft's aspectual classification, including definitions, examples and other names for the aspectual types.

Based on Croft's analysis, we annotated a small sample of sentences from the data from the shared annotation task for the NAACL 2016 4th Workshop on Events (RED annotation), from which we had filtered nonfinite examples (including modals and negatives) and also perfects, whose aspectual analysis is complex, as they represent the midpoint of a grammaticalization path from a resultative state construction to perfective and past event constructions (Bybee et al., 1994; Croft, 2012).

We initially began with a two-level annotation starting from the Vendler classes as in Table 1. However, we found that a more effective annotation began with very common paired (two-way) aspectual ambiguities at the first level. For example *He removed the bones* could be construed as either a directed achievement or an incremental accomplishment. Sentence context cannot always resolve such

Aspectual Ambiguity Class	Aspectual Image Schema	Example
Inceptive State	Transitory State Directed Achievement	*I remember her name.* *Suddenly I remembered her name.*
Expandable Action	Directed Achievement Accomplishment (Incremental/Nonincremental)	*He died at 9:17pm.* *He died in four hours.*
Accomplishable Action	Incremental Accomplishment Directed Activity	*Jules read the magazine (in an hour).* *Jules read the magazine (for an hour).*
Directable Action	Directed Activity Undirected Activity	*He was running down the alley.* *The kids ran all afternoon.*
Cyclic Action	Undirected Activity Cyclic Achievement (Semelfactive)	*The light was flashing.* *The light flashed (once).*
Inactive Action	Undirected Activity Transitory State	*He is tasting the soup.* *I taste the onion in the soup.*
Inherent Action	Inherent State Transitory State	*The statue stands in the main square.* *Joe is standing outside.*
Disposition	Inherent State Undirected Activity	*She is polite.* *She is being polite.*

Table 2: Aspect annotation scheme

ambiguities, but the second level of annotation will be used for such ambiguity resolution where possible (NB: we do not disambiguate reversible and irreversible directed achievements at this stage). The common paired aspectual ambiguities can be observed in a multidimensional scaling analysis of English and Japanese verbal aspectual ambiguities (Croft, 2012, 266). These ambiguities are often not easily resolvable in texts, but the common ambiguities allow us to reduce the annotation possibilities to just two image schemas. The annotation scheme is presented in Table 2.

English is more flexible than other languages in using a single predicate form in more than one aspectual image schema. Other languages use derivational morphology to distinguish different aspectual construals of the same verb; this is true for some English Inactive Actions (*She is sleeping/asleep*. In fact, the paired image schemas in Table 2 understate the range of aspectual construals of English predicates; many predicates allow more than two construals. The multidimensional scaling analysis in Croft (2012) implies the semantic map of aspectual ambiguities in Figure 1. A predicate is likely to allow aspectual ambiguity in two or more connected aspectual image schemas in this semantic map. Our admittedly small sample suggests that although a verb out of sentence context may be multiply ambiguous aspectually, a verb in a specific sentence context may be only pairwise ambiguous, or not ambiguous at all, most of the time.

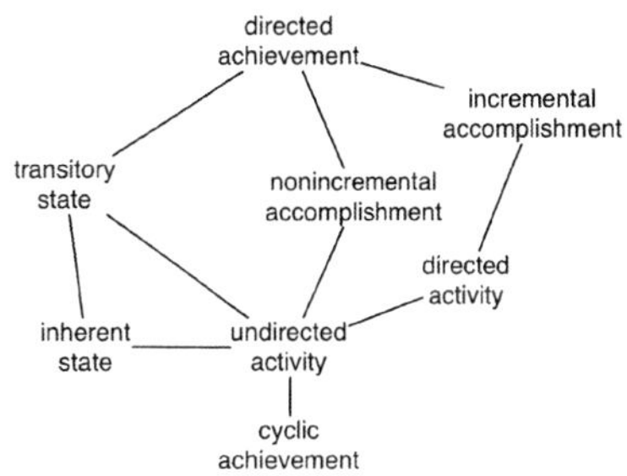

Figure 1: Semantic map of common aspectual ambiguities

Croft (2012) supports his classification of aspectual types by presenting a phasal analysis of events mapped on two geometric dimensions, time (t) and qualitative state (q). These phases generate the aspectual types listed in Table 1. The basic phases Croft posits are:

- states, having one point on q persisting for different temporal durations (point, finite segment, and a segment extending to the end of the entity's timeline for permanent and inherent states);
- transitions, for punctual changes of state on q;

- a monotonic function on q for directed activities/incremental accomplishments; and
- a nonmonotonic function on q for undirected activities/nonincremental accomplishments.

A simple verb in a particular tense-aspect construction generally designates or *profiles* (Langacker, 1987) one phase. Other phases are also represented if they are presupposed, such as the initial rest state and inception of an event, or entailed, such as the result state of an achievement or accomplishment. Accomplishments profile the inception and completion phases as well, since they are temporally and qualitatively bounded events. Croft's graphic representations of two examples of the aspectual types in Table 2 are given in Figure 2:

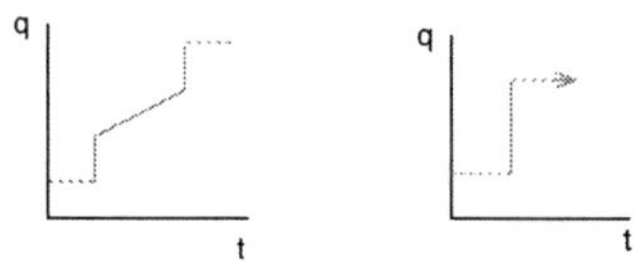

Figure 2: Aspectual representation of an incremental accomplishment and an irreversible directed achievement

The incremental accomplishment includes five phases (in blue): the rest state, the inception transition, the directed change, the completion transition and the (transitory) result state. The directed change and the transitions that bound it are profiled. The directed achievement consists only of the rest state, the transition, and the permanent result state; and only the transition is profiled.

Croft's graphic representations of aspectual phases need to be formalized in order to allow for temporal reasoning over the aspectual analysis of events in a text. There are several possibilities that we are currently exploring. All involve a temporal interval logic (Allen, 1984) for the time dimension. States and changes of state on the q dimension can be modeled using Dynamic Interval Temporal Logic (Pustejovsky and Moszkowicz, 2011), or by a point- or vector-based model.

3 Annotation of force-dynamic event structure for physical events

We present an annotation scheme for physical events that is novel but derived from linguistic research that argues that events in simple clauses are analyzed in terms of causal transmission of force interactions between participants in the event (Talmy, 1976; Talmy, 1988; Croft, 1991; Croft, 2012). We briefly summarize the transmission of force model before introducing our annotation scheme and its linguistic justification.

The concept of causation in mind here is the narrow one pertaining to commonsense reasoning and lexical semantics called intrinsic causation by Ikuta et al. (2014), a local relation between events, not the broader causal complex (Hobbs, 2005) including all enabling conditions that must hold in order for a result to occur. Talmy (1976) develops the common "billiard ball" model of causation (Langacker, 1991) in which one participant forcefully acts on a second participant leading to some sort of change in the Agonist. Talmy (1976) defines four types of causation: *physical*, the basic physical force transmission relation; *volitional*, where an agent volitionally acts on a physical entity; *affective*, where an external entity causes a change in mental state; and *inducive*, where an agent volitionally causes a change in mental state of another agent through social interaction (communication, authority, etc.). In the following example, the force transmission from Sue to the hammer is volitional causation, from the hammer to the coconut is physical causation, and from the coconut's breaking to Greg's satisfaction is affective causation:

(4) Sue broke the coconut for Greg with a hammer.

Sue → *hammer* → *coconut* → *Greg*
VOL PHYS AFF

Croft (1991) also extends Talmy's force transmission analysis to noncausal relations, such as the spatial relation between the paint (spatial figure) and the wall (ground) in the well-known *spray/load* alternation (*Jack sprayed paint on the wall/Jack sprayed the wall with paint*). Both sentences describe a situation in which Jack causes paint to end up on the wall. There is a semantic difference, best analyzed by Dowty (1991): the progress of the event is measured out by the change undergone by the direct object participant (the incremental theme). In the first example, the event is measured out by the paint going onto the wall; in the second example, the event is measured out by the wall getting covered by the paint.

Croft's model allows us to decompose events into a causal chain. However, Croft's causal model only describes who is acting on whom. It is too schematic to capture the more fine-grained categories of events that are assumed in discussions of verbs, argument structure constructions and their associated meanings by linguists such as Goldberg and Levin and Rappaport Hovav. We propose a force dynamic annotation scheme that captures these finer-grained distinctions; at this stage, it applies to physical interactions among physical entities, possibly brought about by agents. The decompositional analysis of force-dynamic image schemas underlying our annotation scheme is based on types of force-dynamic interactions proposed by Talmy (1988) and on types of incremental themes proposed by Dowty (1991), Tenny (1994), Hay et al. (1999), and others. Table 3 gives the force-dynamic image schemas that we posit; names for event types in the linguistics literature subsumed by these schemas are given in italics.

The distinction between Force/Resist and the remaining force dynamic image schemas in Table 3 is based on the analysis of force dynamics in Talmy (1988). Talmy proposes a model of causal interactions that is generalized from the "billiard ball" model; Talmy calls the transmitter of force the *Antagonist*, and the receiver of force the *Agonist*. In the "billiard ball" model, the Agonist has a tendency towards stasis, the Antagonist a tendency towards change, and the outcome of the force-dynamic interaction is change (of the Agonist). Talmy contrasts this with other possible combinations of participant tendency and outcome. In cases of simple contact and force exertion, such as *He tapped the windowpane* or *They pushed the door (and it didn't budge)*, the Agonist tends towards stasis and the Antagonist towards change, as in "billiard ball" causation; but the outcome is stasis (that is, the Agonist is largely unchanged). In cases of maintaining or resisting, as in *She was holding a ball*, the force dynamics is the inverse: the Agonist (the ball) tends towards change (falling), but the Antagonist tends towards stasis, and the outcome is stasis. These nonprototypical force-dynamic image schemas, where the outcome is stasis rather than change, will be called Force and Resist respectively.

The remaining force-dynamic image schemas in Table 3 are all subtypes of "billiard ball" causation. They are distinguished primarily by the type of scale on the qualitative dimension that the "theme" entity undergoes. Scales may be incremental or instantaneous (Croft, 2012; Beavers, 2013). For incremental changes, some linguists have argued that all such changes be analyzed as mereological: change proceeds part by part, as in *I mowed the lawn* (Krifka, 1989; Krifka, 1998; Dowty, 1991). Hay et al. (1999) have argued that all such changes be analyzed as scalar change of a property of an entity, as in *The balloon expanded.* Croft (2012) argues that mereological change and property change are two different types of incremental change, along with two other incremental changes discussed by Dowty (1991): holistic themes, when an entity gradually moves on a path; and representation-source themes, when the incremental change is defined on a source, as in *I copied the book.* Instantaneous changes also fall into the same four types (Croft, 2012).

Property theme change, as in *The balloon rose* or *The soup cooled*, constitutes the change of state force dynamic image schema. Path theme change is found in all the different types of motion events, such as *The car screeched around the corner* or *She tapped the ball into the pocket.*

Mereological theme change constitutes the largest number of image schemas. One scheme, which we will call Application as in *She wiped polish onto the table*, describes putting a figure entity on (or in) a ground entity. Hence Application includes putting, inserting, combining and mixing; these differences are encoded by the verb, not the force dynamics. Its reverse (Cruse, 1973) is Removal (including separating), as in *She wiped the dust off the table.* Another related scheme, Covering as in *He sprayed the wall with paint*, describes incrementally covering (or filling) a ground entity with a figure entity. These alternating schemas differ in that Application treats the figure as the incremental theme while Covering treats the ground as the incremental theme (Dowty, 1991). They are treated as distinct frames by Fillmore and Atkins (1992) and Baker and Ruppenhofer (2002). The reverse of Covering is Uncovering (including emptying), as in *I stripped the trees of bark.*

The fourth type of theme, the representation-source theme, applies exclusively to replication. But

	Direct	**Inverse**
	Force (*contact, force exertion*)	Resist (*maintain*)
Theme	**Direct**	**Reverse**
Property	Change of State	
Path	Motion (*directed motion, manner of motion*)	
Mereological	Apply (*application, combining*)	Remove (*removal, separation*)
	Cover (*covering, filling*)	Uncover (*uncovering, emptying*)
Design	Create	Destroy
	Transform	
	Replicate	
Possession	Transfer	Obtain

Table 3: Force-dynamic image schemas

replication semantically belongs to a family of event types including creation, transformation and destruction that all involve changes to the categorial identity and/or individual integrity of the theme entity.

One characteristic of this family of event types is that the events are often not incremental. For example in creation (writing, composing, painting), one revises, deletes and reorganizes (Rothstein, 2004). Also, if part of a window cracks, it is construed as broken, even if later the crack lengthens or additional cracks appear. Some creation processes such as baking bread involve different types of processes such as mixing ingredients together, letting it sit, and heating it in the oven; this process cannot be described as simply mereological or a property change. These processes all involve following a design, as in a recipe. In replication, the design is simply the structure of the source; in transformation and creation, the design is in the creator's mind, and may be more of a process like a recipe than a pre-formed product. Destruction is the reverse of creation: undoing a design. We will call this generalization of the representation-source theme a *design theme*.

Finally, transfer and obtaining involve a change in possession, a socially-defined characteristic of physical objects (and other entities).

The first level of force dynamic annotation, given in Table 3, provides the type of the "core" interaction in a single-clause event. In simple clauses, the "core" force dynamic interaction can be supplemented by an external cause (typically volitional or inducive causation) antecedent to the core interaction, and by a beneficiary (affective causation) subsequent to the core interaction. The second level of force dynamic annotation that we propose involves the presence, if any, of additional participants in the causal chain, namely a causer and/or a beneficiary; and whether or not the event profile includes the initiator (usually the agent) or not, the latter case being the grammatically distinct passive argument structure construction with an oblique initiator. The additional annotation has a combination of any or all or none of the values causer, beneficiary and passive.

A preliminary annotation of a set of sentences from the NAACL 2016 4th Workshop on Events data (RED annotation) began by filtering out events in VerbNet classes for which we have not developed force-dynamic image schemas. We then annotated verbs whose VerbNet class allows more than one force-dynamic image schema: *9. Putting* (Apply or Cover image schemas), *10. Removing* (Remove or Uncover image schemas), *11. Sending and Carrying* (Motion or Transfer), and *26. Creation and Transformation* (Create or Transform). Unlike the aspectual annotation, here we concluded that the verbs in the corpus were largely unambiguous as to their force-dynamic image schema, and can be disambiguated using suitable annotation guidelines. Our work with force-dynamic image schemas is much less advanced than the analysis of aspectual image schemas, which are also smaller in number. As we scale up with a fuller set of force-dynamic image schemas, the annotation schema is likely to evolve beyond the simple scheme in Table 3.

The finer-grained force-dynamic annotation, combined with the finer-grained aspectual annotation described in section 2, can be translated into the causal-aspectual event structures described in this paper, and then used for semantic analysis and inference about events and their participants. Croft (2012) integrates the phasal aspectual decomposition of an event with the causal chain decomposition of the same event. An example of Croft's integrated graphic representation for *Jane mowed the lawn* is given in Figure 3. Croft decomposes the event into subevents each of which has its own participant. This decomposition allows the integration of Talmy's model of transmission of force between participants and the standard model of causation as events causing other events. What one participant does/undergoes causes another participant to do/undergo something in the event. The graphic representation aligns each participant's subevent temporally, and places the causally antecedent participant below the subsequent participant.

Each participant performs/undergoes its own subevent, represented by the blue *t/q* aspectual representations as in Figure 2, associated with Jane and the lawn. The red vertical arrows represent the force-dynamic interaction between participants (Jane's mowing causes the lawn to be mowed—a mereological change) that is encoded by the verb and argument structure construction. The labels 'mow' and 'mown' are a shorthand for the undirected activity of Jane and the mereological incremental accomplishment of the lawn. The italicized forms indicate the words associated with components of the graphic representation, and the capitalized terms represent the argument phrases of the argument structure construction.

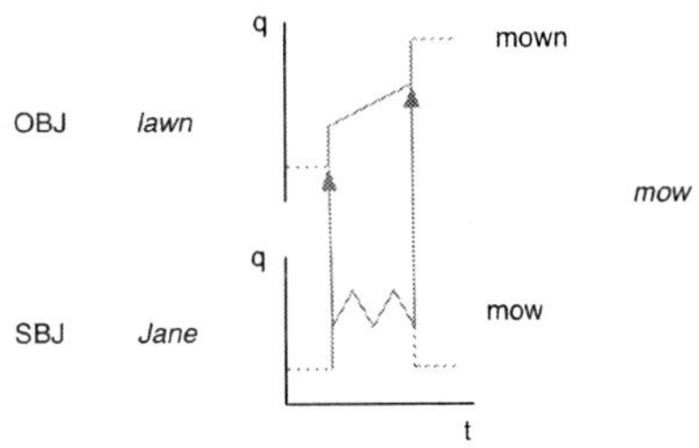

Figure 3: A representation of an aspectual and causal event decomposition.

Again, Croft's representations need to be formalized in order to allow for casual reasoning over the force-dynamic analyses of events in a text. We are looking into dynamic graph structure (Harary and Gupta, 1997), which incorporates a temporal dimension through which force-dynamic interactions between individuals change, as well as the qualitative features of those individuals (namely the q dimension); or a vector model of force dynamics similar to the model proposed by Warglien et al. (2012).

4 Conclusion

At this point, the annotation scheme is only a proposal based on the decompositional semantic analysis of event structure presented in this paper. The annotation scheme will continue to be field-tested to report on standard measures of inter-annotator agreement for the subset of physical events that it intends to capture. Provided that is successful, the annotation scheme will then be extended to other event types than those accounted for here. Several other physical force-dynamic image schemas must be analyzed. Emission and ingestion involve creation/destruction of the Agonist by the Antagonist, but also motion of the Agonist relative to the Antagonist. Existence and other unary valency events do not involve force-dynamic interactions, but do involve a variety of participant theme types. Other force-dynamic image schemas involve interactions between nondistinct participants, such as a human and her or his body part, and reflexive and reciprocal interactions, including the commercial transaction frame. Finally, there are also "mental dynamics", in which the interaction involves mental states or processes, and "social dynamics", in which the interaction involves social relationships and statuses.

More broadly, the decompositional analysis of monoclausal events will allow us to integrate the temporal and causal relations within monoclausal events and temporal and causal relations between events expressed in separate clauses. The result of this analysis will be a "least common denominator" description of events and event relationships that is invariant as to how events are linguistically expressed (one clause or multiple clauses), and a means to translate from linguistic expressions to this basic description of events. Using this decomposition, we can model the events reported in a text as a dynamic evolving network of individual entities, each of which is changing over time and interacting with other entities in the network, causally or in other ways.

References

James F. Allen. 1984. Towards a general theory of action and time. *Artificial Intelligence*, 23:123–54.

Collin F. Baker and Josef Ruppenhofer. 2002. FrameNet's frames vs. Levin's verb classes. In Julie Larson and Mary Paster, editors, *Proceedings of the Twenty-eighth Annual Meeting of the Berkeley Linguistics Society*, pages 27–38. Berkeley: Berkeley Linguistics Society.

Laura Banarescu, Claire Bonial, Shu Cau, Madalina Georgescu, Kira Griffitt, Ulf Hermjakob, Kevin Knight, Phillipp Koehn, Martha Palmer, and Nathan Schneider. 2013. Abstract meaning representation for Sembanking. In *Proceedings of the 7th Linguistic Annotation Workshop*.

John Beavers. 2013. Aspectual classes and scales of change. *Linguistics*, 51:681–706.

Pier Marco Bertinetto and Mario Squartini. 1995. An attempt at defining the class of 'gradual completion verbs'. In Pier Marco Bertinetto, Valentina Bianchi, James Higginbotham, and Mario Squartini, editors, *Temporal reference, aspect and actionality*, volume 1, pages 11–26. Torino: Rosenberg and Sellier.

Joan L. Bybee, Revere D. Perkins, and William Pagliuca. 1994. *The evolution of grammar: tense, aspect and modality in the languages of the world.* Chicago: University of Chicago Press.

Gregory N. Carlson. 1979. Generics and atemporal when. *Linguistics and Philosophy*, 3:49–98.

William Croft. 1991. *Syntactic categories and grammatical relations: the cognitive organization of information.* Chicago: University of Chicago Press.

William Croft. 1998. Event structure in argument linking. In Miriam Butt and Wilhelm Geuder, editors, *The projection of arguments: lexical and compositional factors*, pages 21–63. Stanford: Center for the Study of Language and Information.

William Croft. 2012. *Verbs: aspect and causal structure.* Oxford University Press.

D. Alan Cruse. 1973. Some thoughts on agentivity. *Journal of Linguistics*, 9:11–23.

David Dowty. 1979. *Word meaning and Montague grammar.* Dordrech: Kluwer.

David Dowty. 1991. Thematic proto-roles and argument selection. *Language*, 67:547–619.

Charles J. Fillmore and B. T. S. Atkins. 1992. Towards a frame-based lexicon: the semantics of risk and its neighbors. In Adrienne Lehrer and Eva Feder Kittay, editors, *Frames, fields and contrasts: new essays in semantics and lexical organization*, pages 75–102. Hillsdale, N. J.: Lawrence Erlbaum Associates.

Charles J. Fillmore, Christopher R. Johnson, and Miriam R. Petruck. 2003. Background to FrameNet. *International Journal of Lexicography*, 16:235–50.

Annemarie Friedrich and Alexis Palmer. 2014. Automatic prediction of aspectual class of verbs in context. In *Proceedings of the 52nd annual meeting of the association for computational linguistics (Short Papers)*, volume 517-523. Association for Computational Linguistics.

Frank Harary and Gopal Gupta. 1997. Dynamic graph models. *Mathematical and Computer Modelling*, 25(7):79–87.

Jennifer Hay, Christopher Kennedy, and Beth Levin. 1999. Scalar structure underlies telicity in "degree achievements". In Tanya Matthews and Devon Strolovitch, editors, *Proceedings of SALT*, volume 9, pages 127–144. Ithaca: Cornell University Press.

Jerry R. Hobbs. 2005. Toward a useful concept of causality for lexical semantics. *Journal of Semantics*, 22:181–209.

Rei Ikuta, William F. Styler, Mariah Hamang, Tim O'Gorman, and Martha Palmer. 2014. Challenges of adding causation to richer event descriptions. In *Proceedings of the 2nd Workshop on EVENTS: Definition, Detection, Conference, and Representation*, pages 12–20. Association for Computational Linguistics.

Ray Jackendoff. 1991. Parts and boundaries. *Cognition*, 41:9–45.

Karin Kipper, Anna Korhonen, Neville Ryant, and Martha Palmer. 2007. A large-scale classification of English verbs. *English Resources and Evaluations*, 42:21–40.

Manfred Krifka. 1989. Nominal reference, temporal constitution, and quantification in event semantics. In Johan van Benthem Renate Bartsch and Peter van Emde Boas, editors, *Semantics and contextual expression*, pages 75–115. Foris: Dordrecht.

Manfred Krifka. 1998. The origins of telicity. In Susan Rothstein, editor, *Events and grammar*, pages 197–235. Dordrech: Kluwer.

Ronald W. Langacker. 1987. *Foundations of Cognitive Grammar, vol. I: theoretical prerequisites.* Stanford: Stanford University Press.

Ronald W. Langacker. 1991. *Foundations of Cognitive Grammar, vol. II: descriptive application.* Stanford: Stanford University Press.

Beth Levin and Malka Rappaport Hovav. 2005. *Argument realization.* Cambridge: Cambridge University Press.

Inderjeet Mani and James Pustejovsky. 2012. *Interpreting motion: grounded representations for spatial language.* Oxford University Press.

Thomas Mathew and Graham E. Katz. 2009. Supervised categorization for habitual versus episodic sentences. In *Sixth Midwest Computational Linguistics Colloquium*. Bloomington, Indiana: Indiana University Press.

Anita Mittwoch. 1988. Aspects of English aspect: on the interaction of perfect, progressive and durational phrases. *Linguistics and Philosophy*, 11:203–54.

Marc Moens and Mark Steedman. 1988. Temporal ontology and temporal reference. *Computational Linguistics*, 14:15–28.

Martha Palmer, Daniel Gildea, and Paul Kingsbury. 2005. The Proposition Bank: an annotated corpus of semantic roles. *Computational Linguistics*, 31(1):71–106.

James Pustejovsky and Jessica L. Moszkowicz. 2011. The qualitative spatial dynamics of motion in language. *Spatial Cognition and Computation*, 11:15–44.

Susan Rothstein. 2004. *Structuring events*. Oxford: Blackwell.

Eric V. Siegel and Kathleen R. McKeown. 2001. Learning methods to combine linguistic indicators: improving aspectual classification and revealing linguistic insights. *Computational Linguistics*, 26(4):595–628.

Carlota Smith. 1991. *The parameter of aspect*. Dordrech: Kluwer.

Leonard Talmy. 1976. Semantic causative types. In Masayoshi Shibatani, editor, *The grammar of causative constructions*, volume 6, pages 43–116. New York: Academic Press.

Leonard Talmy. 1985. Lexicalization patterns: semantic structure in lexical forms. In Timothy Shopen, editor, *Language typology and syntactic description: grammatical categories and the lexicon*, volume 3, pages 57–149. Cambridge: Cambridge University Press.

Leonard Talmy. 1988. Force dynamics in language and cognition. *Cognitive Science*, 2:49–100.

Carol L. Tenny. 1994. *Aspectual roles and the syntax-semantics interface*. Dordrech: Kluwer.

Robert D. Van Valin and Randy J. LaPolla. 1997. *Syntax: structure, meaning and function*. Cambridge: Cambridge University Press.

Zeno Vendler. 1957. Verbs and times. *The Philosophical Review*, 66:143–60.

Massimo Warglien, Peter Gärdenfors, and Matthijs Westera. 2012. Event structure, conceptual spaces and the semantics of verbs. *Theoretical Linguistics*, 38:159–93.

Nianwen Xue and Yuchen Zhang. 2014. Buy one get one free: distant annotation of Chinese tense, event type, and modality. In *Proceedings of the 9th International Conference on Languages Resources and Evaluation (LREC-2014)*, pages 1412–1416. European Language Resources Association.

Alessandra Zarcone and Alessandro Lenci. 2008. Computational models of event type classification in context. In *Proceedings of the 6th International Conference on Language Resources and Evaluation (LREC 08)*, pages 1232–1238. European Language Resources Association.

Multimodal Use of an Upper-Level Event Ontology

Claire Bonial,[1] David Tahmoush,[1] Susan Windisch Brown,[2] and Martha Palmer[2]
[1]U.S. Army Research Lab, Adelphi, Maryland
[2]University of Colorado, Boulder, Boulder, Colorado
Claire.N.Bonial.civ@mail.mil, David.Tahmoush.civ@mail.mil
Susan.Brown@colorado.edu, Martha.Palmer@colorado.edu

Abstract

We describe the ongoing development of a lexically-informed, upper-level event ontology and explore use cases of the ontology. This ontology draws its lexical sense distinctions from VerbNet, FrameNet and the Rich Entities, Relations and Events Project. As a result, the ontology facilitates interoperability and the combination of annotations done for each independent resource. While this ontology is intended to be practical for a variety of applications, here we take the initial steps in determining whether or not the event ontology could be utilized in multimodal applications, specifically to recognize and reason about events in both text and video. We find that the ontology facilitates the generalization of potentially noisy or sparse individual realizations of events into larger categories of events and enables reasoning about event relations and participants, both of which are useful in event recognition and interpretation regardless of modality.

1 Introduction & Background

The valuable computational lexical resources, VerbNet (Kipper et al., 2008), FrameNet (Fillmore et al., 2002), and the Rich Entities, Relations and Events (ERE) annotation project (Song et al., 2015), each provide somewhat distinct information about which eventualities are related syntactically, semantically, or both, and which types of participants are involved in classes of eventualities. VerbNet and FrameNet also involve long-standing and comprehensive annotation efforts, using the class and participant type labels set out in each resource. The resulting annotated corpora have proved to be useful sources of training data for a variety of Natural Language Processing (NLP) systems, including automatic semantic role labeling, word sense disambiguation, and question-answering systems.

Recently, we have also seen an expansion of efforts in both the construction of ontologies as part of the Semantic Web (Berners-Lee, 1998), and research in computer vision (e.g., Fei-Fei & Perona, 2005). These previously disparate threads of research have begun to come together with NLP research in fruitful ways. First, there have been efforts to integrate computational lexical resources into the Semantic Web (e.g., Eckle-Kohler et al., 2014). Progress in this area, however, has been somewhat slow and difficult, given that conversion of resources like FrameNet, which includes quite nuanced and complex ontological relations, into the minimalist Resource Descriptive Framework (RDF) schema used in the Semantic Web is not necessarily a trivial conversion and may involve some loss of information (e.g., Nuzzolese et al., 2011; Scheffczyk et al., 2006). Second, data-driven methods for extracting events from text are increasingly being combined with knowledge-driven methods, such as those based on ontologies, in order to benefit from the strengths of both (Hogenboom et al., 2011). Third, there have been efforts to use both text and visual data jointly to interpret complex scenes (e.g.,

Proceedings of the 4th Workshop on Events: Definition, Detection, Coreference, and Representation, pages 18–26,
San Diego, California, June 17, 2016.

Karpathy et al., 2014). Furthermore, we have seen the promise of integrating ontological information into computer vision research evidenced in the success of ImageNet (Deng et al., 2009), a large-scale ontology of images built upon the structure of WordNet (Fellbaum, 1998).

To further exploit and encourage synergy in all of these research areas, both language processing, vision processing, and the marriage of the two, our goal is to create an upper-level event ontology that provides conceptual coverage for the aforementioned lexical resources, and uses them as the sense inventories that house the linguistic realizations of those concepts in English. This ontology is being developed with multi-modal applications in mind, and in this research we explore the utility of the ontology in a text-processing application as well as a video-processing application. The primary motivations for developing this ontology are two-fold: first, as with most ontologies, the event ontology should allow for reasoning about events and their participants, with a special focus on temporal and causal relations between events. Second, the event ontology should allow for the generalization of specific events, allowing for the detection of similar events in text and facilitating the recognition of the same action being performed by different people under different circumstances in video. The latter aim is especially challenging given that we cannot assume that the level of generalization appropriate for text applications would be the same for video applications.

In this paper, we describe the current structure of the ontology, which is still under development, including a brief description of the resources we are drawing upon for sense distinctions and for temporal and causal relations. The ontology will be openly released to the research community, but is not yet available given that it is still undergoing changes and expansions. Next, we describe preliminary efforts to explore both text and video use cases of the ontology. Pertaining to text, we focus on connecting two different descriptions of the same event via lexical similarity, such as *seize* and *capture*. Next, we examine the feasibility of using ontological relations to improve human activity recognition in videos, focusing on the detection of *pick up and throw* activities, which often occur sequentially.

2 Event Ontology Design

To facilitate compatibility with the Semantic Web, our ontology is being developed using the open-source ontology editor, Protégé (Noy et al., 2000), in OWL format. An early design decision we faced was how to incorporate the lexicons of interest into an ontology. The approach we have chosen is to develop and maintain VerbNet and FrameNet, and the ERE event types as distinct, stand-alone ontologies that are imported into the upper-level event ontology. The individual lexicons and the ontology are linked through the "has_Sense" relation: conceptual nodes in the ontology have senses and associated lexical items spelled out in the lexicons.

2.1 Sense Inventories

Currently, we have successfully implemented both VerbNet and ERE in OWL, since these lexicons have only very shallow hierarchical class structures. However, we are still developing the OWL-implementation of FrameNet, since, as mentioned previously, the ontological structure and inheritance types in FrameNet are quite complex. To this point, we have been developing the FrameNet lexical ontology on an as-needed basis, and including only basic inheritance links within the FrameNet ontology. However, we are exploring the feasibility of adopting an existing OWL-implementation of FrameNet (e.g., Scheffczyk et al., 2006), and importing this directly into the upper-level ontology. Brief descriptions of each of the lexical resources included in the ontology are given below, with explanations of how the sense distinctions vary across each resource.

VerbNet, based on the work of Levin (1993), groups verbs into "classes" based on compatibility with certain "diathesis alternations" or syntactic alternations (e.g., *She loaded the wagon with hay* vs. *She loaded hay into the wagon*). Although the groupings are primarily syntactic, the classes do share semantic features as well, since, as Levin posited, the syntactic behavior of a verb is largely determined by its meaning.

VerbNet includes a semantic representation for each usage example demonstrating a characteristic diathesis alternation of a class. For example, in the Throw class, the following alternate is listed with its semantic representation, based on individual semantic predicates (e.g., **motion, cause, exert_force**):

Example: "Steve tossed the ball to the garden."
Roles: Agent Verb Theme Destination
Semantic Predicates
EXERT_FORCE(during(E0), Agent, Theme)
CONTACT(during(E0), Agent, Theme)
MOTION(during(E1), Theme)
not(CONTACT(during(E1), Agent, Theme))
not(LOCATION(start(E1), Theme, Destination))
LOCATION(end(E1), Theme, Destination)
CAUSE(Agent, E1)
meets(E0, E1)

This representation is intended to break the event down into smaller semantic elements, given as the predicates. The predicates are organized with respect to the time of the event (designated as 'E'); thus they can apply *during,* at the *start* or at the *end* of an event. Although somewhat complex for this event, the above representation is meant to capture the fact that Steve (Agent) is in contact with and exerts force on a ball (Theme); he then releases (is not in contact with) the ball and the ball is in motion; the ball's location at the end of the motion event is at the garden (Destination), where it was not located at the start of the event; Steve causes this event as the Agent having thrown the ball. Notice that although this semantic interpretation captures many of the salient semantic components of a throwing event, it may not capture the salient *visual* aspects of a throwing event, which may stem more from the sequential motions of the body and body parts.

Within the ontology, VerbNet will serve as a lexicon imported into the ontology, and it will therefore provide one set of sense distinctions for the English lexical items that denote concepts within the ontology. Because class membership in VerbNet is in part based on syntactic information, VerbNet captures the level of sense distinctions that are clearly evidenced by differences in syntactic behaviors.

FrameNet, based on Fillmore's frame semantics (Fillmore, 1976; Fillmore & Baker, 2001), groups verbs, nouns and adjectives into "frames" based on words or "frame elements" that evoke the same semantic frame: a description of a type of event, relation, or entity and the participants in it. For example, the Apply_heat frame includes the frame elements Cook, Food, Heating_instrument, Temperature_setting, etc. The "net" of frames makes up a rather complex ontological network, including simple "is_A" inheritance relations as well as more complex relations such as Precedes and Perspective_on. FrameNet will serve as another lexicon within the ontology, providing a different set of sense distinctions for the lexical items denoting concepts. Since the classification of FrameNet is purely semantic and based on shared frame elements, the sense distinctions and distinctions between participant types made in FrameNet are often more fine-grained than VerbNet. For example, given the sentence *Sally fried an egg*, VerbNet would label *Sally* with the traditional semantic role label Agent, while FrameNet would label *Sally* with the more semantically specified label of Cook.

The Rich Entities, Relations, and Events (ERE) project is based on the Automatic Content Extraction (ACE) project's semantic role annotation schema (Doddington et al., 2004). The goal of the ERE project is to mark up the events (and other types of relations; i.e. "eventualities") and the entities involved in them, and to mark coreference between these. This provides a somewhat shallow representation of the meaning of the text. The ERE schema will also serve as a sort of lexicon imported into the ontology, with its event type and subtype designations serving as links to the lexical items marked up with that designation. ERE annotated eventualities are limited to certain types and subtypes of special interest within the defense community, with top-level types referred to as *Life, Movement, Transaction, Business, Conflict, Manufacture, Contact, Personnel* and *Justice* events. Thus, the sense distinctions made by this resource are grounded in practical considerations of what event types are deemed to be of interest, and therefore offer very different insights and information into related events when compared with either FrameNet or VerbNet.

2.2 Ontology Structure & Relations

There are many critical decisions to be made when determining what concepts and relations to represent in an ontology; thus, we draw upon the decisions made in the established ontologies WordNet

(Fellbaum, 1998), the Suggested Upper Merged Ontology, SUMO (Pease, 2002), the Descriptive Ontology for Linguistic and Cognitive Engineering, DOLCE (Masolo et al., 2003), and The Basic Formal Ontology, BFO (Smith & Grenon, 2002). Similar to the structures of each of these existing ontologies, we have selected a top level concept, Entity, with an initial distinction between Endurant and Perdurant entities. Borrowing heavily from DOLCE, we have developed the following definitions. We define "Entity" as *a unique object or set of objects in the world – for instance a specific person, place or organization – that typically functions as a participant.* We define "Endurants" as *those entities that can be observed/perceived as a complete concept, no matter which given snapshot of time – were we to freeze time, we would still be able to perceive the entire endurant.* We define "Perdurants" as *those entities for which only a part exists if we look at them at any given snapshot in time. Variously called events, processes phenomena, or activities and states, perdurants have temporal parts or spatial parts and participants.*

We also need to capture richer information about the temporal and causal relations between events than any of the lexical resources described thus far are currently capturing independently. To ensure that the ontology captures temporal and causal relations of utility within NLP, we use relations from the established Richer Event Description (RED) project (Ikuta et al., 2014). Like ERE, the RED project also aims to markup text with mentions of eventualities and entities, but the primary focus of RED is to represent the temporal and causal relationships between those eventualities. The final goal is to produce annotations rich enough that a computer, using complex inferencing, co-reference, and domain-specific algorithms, would be able to construct an accurate timeline of when the events in a given document occur relative to any fixed dates present and relative to one another (e.g., automatically constructed timelines of medical histories). RED builds on THYME (Styler et al., 2014), a temporal relationship annotation of clinical data that is based on TimeML (Pustejovsky et al., 2010). The temporal relations are quite fine-grained, including *Before, Before+overlap, Overlap, and CONTAIN.* These labels are further distinguished with causal labels where appropriate: *Before/Causes, Before/Preconditions.* To anchor the events into a timeline, RED links the event to a document time or section time where applicable, and marks up explicit references to time in the document.

2.3 Snapshot of the Ontology

The construction of the ontology is still underway, and has involved a combination of bottom-up and top-down approaches. As ERE event types provide useful constraints on which events to focus on initially, our efforts generally begin with an examination of a particular ERE event type, a comparison of sense distinctions and associated lexical items made in VerbNet and FrameNet, followed by a preliminary fleshing-out of one area of the ontology. At this point, we have situated the top level ERE event types *Life, Conflict, Contact, Justice* and *Personnel.* Thus, we have also situated most of the subtypes within these event types, although our approach involves some iterative refinement of the ontology's class structure.

A simple example portion of the ontology, with sense mappings to VerbNet only, is shown in Figure 1. Within each of the lexical classes, the individual lexical items denoting senses of a concept are listed within each resource. For example, the VerbNet Birth class lists the lexical items *bear, birth, deliver, father, mother, sire, spawn,* etc. The parallel FrameNet Being_born frame includes just *born* and the phrase *come into the world.* ERE realizations include any lexical item tagged as a trigger indicating this type of event during annotation, such as the verb *born* and the noun *birth.*

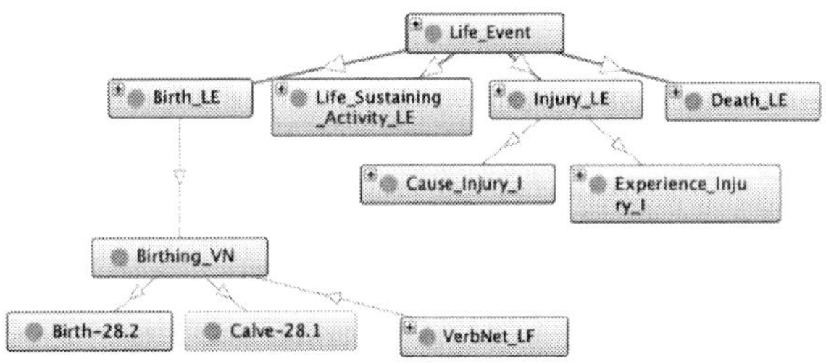

Figure 1: Life_Event extract of event ontology.

Events within the ontology are also related via temporal and causal relations, such as "has_Result" and "has_Precondition." Here, for example, Birth life events are linked to the Life state, Alive (a daughter node to Stative_Perdurant), through the "has_Result" link: once something is born, it is alive. While some of these relations have been developed (and are still under development) specifically for the upper-level ontology, other relations stem directly from the RED project.

3 Use Cases

As mentioned above, the desire to robustly identify and corefer events, either in text or in video, is a primary motivating factor for our development of the ontology. We also wish to be able to reason about the events detected, and draw plausible inferences. Both of these goals require a level of abstraction that can facilitate the detection of two different instances of the same event, whether they are textual or visual. For instance, textual event descriptions may use quite different language, such as *Stock prices rose precipitously*, and *The Stock Market leapt ahead.* Visual events might have different types of agents, performing the same action in different ways. There is preliminary evidence that VerbNet argument structure and semantic predicates can provide a useful level of abstraction, that can serve both language processing and vision processing aims. Prior work demonstrated VerbNet's effectiveness in providing the foundation for Parameterized Action Representations (PARs), a framework for translating verbal instructions into processing commands for a virtual agent (Badler et al., 1999; Badler et al, 2000). The thematic roles indicate the participants in the action, and the semantic predicates help to define the planning goals the virtual agent needs to properly execute the desired action. The level of abstraction encoded in PARs generalized surprisingly well to different sizes and types of agents, simplifying the task of using motion capture to expand the coverage of actions the virual agents could perform (Bindiganavale et al., 2000). The PAR application focuses on the generation of virtual action videos rather than analysis, but it provides encouraging evidence that the same level of abstraction could benefit analysis as well.

In the sections to follow, we introduce the ways in which our ontology and its connections to established lexical resources could be uniquely valuable for both a text and video processing application.

3.1 Text Use Case

For supervised machine learning systems, instances unseen in training data are problematic. Access to related terms found in lexical resources can allow them to generalize training data to additional instances.

Liu et al. (2014) identify problems even with human annotation of events, noting that in the EventCorefBank corpus (Bejan and Harabajiu, 2010), "seizing 12 Somali and 11 Yemeni nationals" and "capturing 23 of the raiders" had not been identified as the same event. Our ontology, in which the lexical items *seize* and *capture* are linked to the same class, could be helpful in automatically connecting these two mentions as the same event. In the discussion of their system of event coreference, Liu et al. also noted that "[event coreference] can possibly be improved by other types of event relations, such as subevent relations." Such relations are an integral part of our event ontology, along with causal, precondition and postcondition relations.

The lexical resources themselves can also be limited in their coverage. For example, consider again the Life_Event portion of the ontology shown in Figure 1. FrameNet lists two entries, *born* and *come into the world* in a frame that would be associated with Birth_LifeEvent. This, too, can lead to data sparsity, but the ontology facilitates pinpointing other lexical items that are more generally related to the entries in FrameNet's semantically fine-grained Being_born frame. Thus, the ontology facilitates some interoperability between the individual lexical resources and makes explicit some of the previously unseen relations between them.

3.2 Video Use Case

Another potential application for an event ontology is for action recognition in video. Human activity recognition has already been explored using images and video. Activity recognition techniques can be grouped into data-driven (Ye et al., 2012) and knowledge-driven (Chen et al., 2012a) approaches. Data-driven techniques use machine learning approaches to discern an activity from the training data. Space-time methods such as space-time volumes, spatio-temporal features, and trajectories have been successful. For classification, generic approaches like support vector machines and hidden Markov models have performed well.

So far, most contestants at a recent Action Classification Challenge at the 2013 International Conference on Computer Vision (ICCV) have utilized low-level features over higher-level class attributes and ontologies because they traditionally have been more effective. Nonetheless, an action ontology can provide a description of the activity using well-structured terminology with a number of properties that are measureable. A well-built ontology could be used, understood, and shared between humans and computers (Gu et al., 2004; Riboni et al., 2009; Chen et al., 2012b) and, as with text applications can facilitate the generalization of specific instances of actions to enable more consistent detection of the same activity, done by different people in different contexts. Furthermore, an action ontology can provide information about the temporal and causal relationships between component actions involved in an activity, potentially improving recognition in ambiguous cases.

In related work, an inventory of attributes of human activities (largely activities related to sports and playing musical instruments) has been developed with a focus on attributes that are visually salient (Jiang et al., 2013). The attributes listed in this resource are quite simple, primarily organized around what body parts are used. For a given action, common attributes of certain body parts or areas of the body are listed for each action (e.g., for *throwing,* Body Part Articulation-Arm = One Arm Raised Head Level).

To a limited extent, these attributes provide a break-down of some of the component parts of an action by detailing some of the ways in which individual body parts move during an activity. However, these attributes are not ordered with respect to time, and many attributes apply throughout an activity instead of expressing finer-grained motions within an activity (e.g., Outdoor). Thus, although this inventory captures many of the aspects of an action that are visually salient, it fails to capture both temporal information and the event-semantics information that is salient in text, which VerbNet's semantic predicates capture.

Therefore, we see an opportunity to explore combining some of these visually salient action attributes with the semantic components of events laid out in VerbNet, and integrating these at the lowest levels of the ontology so that they are clearly temporally and causally related. For example, *throw* events can be broken down into the following time-ordered attributes based on VerbNet semantic predicates (described in Section 2.1):

- Time1: Agent physically grasps Theme – **Contact**(Agent, Theme)
- Time2: Exert force propelling Theme from Agent – **Exert_Force**(Agent, Theme)
- Time3: Release theme – ***not***(**Contact**(Agent, Theme))
- Time4: Theme is in motion – **motion**(Theme)

Situated in the ontology, these attributes would be related via RED temporal/causal relations, making explicit the fact that **Contact** is in a *Before+Overlapping/Preconditions* relation with **Exert_Force**, and that **Exert_Force** is in a *Before/Causes* relation with **Motion.** Admittedly, to break down all events into these smaller components would be a massive undertaking; thus, we would consider only a subset of sufficiently physical actions, and we begin here by simply exploring whether or not breaking down a single complex activity, *pick up and throw*, into its components seems to aid in recognition.

3.2.1 Approach: Skeletonized Video

As mentioned previously, human activity recognition has been explored using images and video, and one benchmark is the MSR-Action3D dataset (Jiang et al., 2013). It includes 20 actions performed by 10 subjects, and each subject performs an action 3 times. An example is shown in Figure 2 for *high wave* where the motion of the arms, legs, head, and torso are shown with the depth dimension removed.

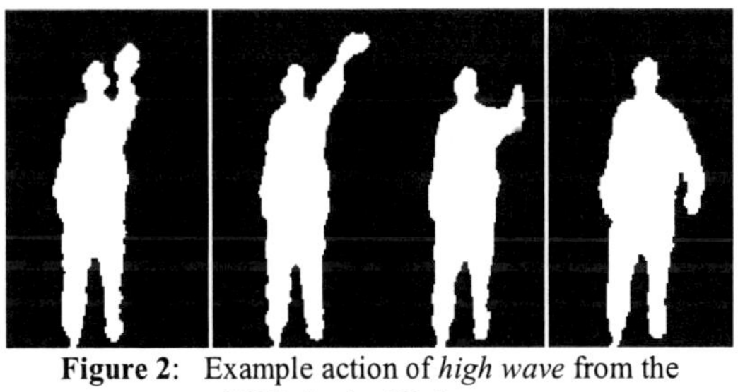

Figure 2: Example action of *high wave* from the MSR-Action3D dataset.

For this work, 20 joint positions are tracked using a skeleton tracker and compiled into a time series of joints *i* depicted as ***pi***(*t*) = (*xi*(*t*); *yi*(*t*); *zi*(*t*)) at a frame *t*. The coordinates are then normalized to reduce dependencies on height, initial body orientation and location. An example of a skeletonized motion is shown in Figure 3.

3.2.2 Preliminary Exploration: Pick Up, Throw

Preliminary work has shown the capability to recognize activities when they are isolated (Tahmoush, 2015). This is similar to recognizing a single word on a piece of paper. However, in longer videos, it is often necessary to segment the video into pieces when there are multiple activities that occur.

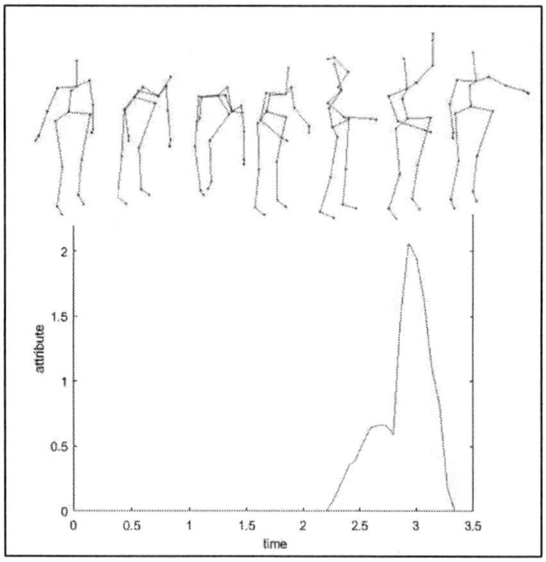

Figure 3: Frames from a skeletonized motion for *pick up and throw* with the measured attribute Body Part Articulation-Arm = One Arm Raised Head Level. Note that the attribute segments out the time period for the *throw* portion.

We look at the compound action of *pick up and throw*, which is part of the MSR-Action3D dataset, which also includes *high throw* and *bend*. When combined, the latter create an activity very similar to *pick up and throw*. In fact, a primary source of misclassifications on this dataset is *pick up and throw* being mistaken for *bend*, as shown in Figure 4.

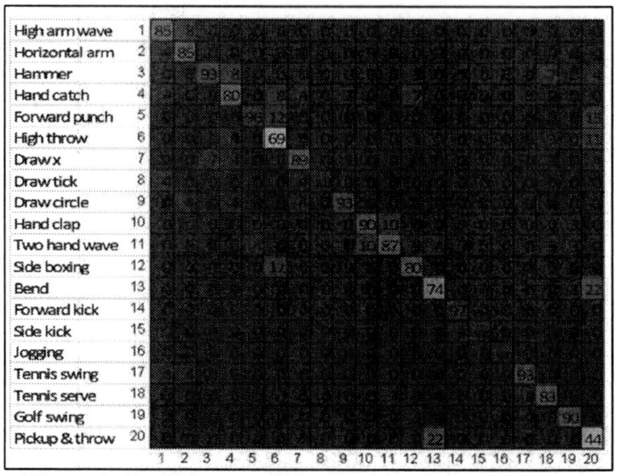

Figure 4: Confusion matrix for activities without using an ontology.

Results of our initial research recognizing smaller activities in larger datasets has shown that motion attributes can perform the important segmentation of videos which can enable improved recognition. In the case of *pick up and throw*, the *throw* activity can be segmented from the *pick up* activity using just one attribute, the Body Part Articulation-Arm = One Arm Raised Head Level attribute that is listed for *throw* (within the previously described Jiang et al. (2013) inventory of attributes). Thus, the use of fast, measurable attributes from an action ontology can effectively segment the video into smaller, more easily recognizable activities without running a costly suite of classifiers. This is illustrated in Figure 3 along with the skeletonized motion.

Our research shows that using the attribute Body Part Articulation-Arm = One Arm Raised Head Level effectively segments the data in 23 out of the 27 *pick up and throw* cases. Visual inspection on the 4 failing cases showed skeletonization failure – the skeletal joints could not be extracted from the video data, thus no skelotonization was produced. Additional visual inspection showed successful segmentation on three cases of *sidearm throwing* and one case of an *underhand toss*, all aberrant cases for *throw* in this data collection. Depending upon how narrowly you define a *throw* action, these could be viewed as false positives. However, this implies both that the attributes allow for some generalization in recognizing *throwing* of all types, and that the attributes may perform well in the case of large variability in the interpretation of the activity.

4 Conclusions & Future Work

An event ontology that could be equally relevant to text processing and language processing would be especially useful for multi-modal processing, and would allow the same generalizations and inferences to be drawn whether the input was textual or visual or both. It is too soon to know if the event ontology described here will achieve that lofty goal, but the possibility is real. In general, we see the potential for ontologies to improve human activity recognition by allowing for more complex actions to be broken down into more easily recognizable activities, as well as easily identifiable, defining attributes of those activities. Therefore, as we further develop the ontology, we are exploring situating fine-grained action attributes within the ontology. Unlike the existing action inventory referenced, this will provide more sophisticated ontological relations, include temporal and causal relations between attributes. We will also continue to explore compatibility with and/or integration of existing ontologies, including Cyc (Reed & Lenat, 2002) and the Emotion Ontology (Hastings et al., 2011).

Acknowledgments

We gratefully acknowledge the support of DARPA DEFT - FA-8750-13-2-0045 and DTRA HDTRA1 -16-1-0002/Project # 1553695, eTASC - Empirical Evidence for a Theoretical Approach to Semantic Components. Any opinions, findings, and conclusions or recommendations expressed in this material are those of the authors and do not necessarily reflect the views of DARPA or the US government.

References

Badler, Norm, Martha Palmer and Rama Bindiganavale. (1999). Animation Control for Real-Time Virtual Humans. *Communications of the ACM. 42(8):65-73.*

Badler, Norm, Rama Bindiganavale, Jan Allbeck, William Schuler, Liwei Zhao, and Martha Palmer. (2000). A Parameterized Action Representation for Virtual Human Agents. *Embodied Conversational Agents.* MIT Press, pgs. 256-284.

Berners-Lee, T. (1998). Semantic web road map.

Bejan, C., & Harabagiu, S. (2010). Unsupervised event coreference resolution with rich linguistic features. Proceedings of the 48th Annual Meeting of the Association for the Association for Computational Linguistics(July), 1412–1422.

Bindiganavale, Rama, William Schuler, Jan Allbeck, Norm Badler, Aravind Joshi,and Martha Palmer. (2000). Dynamically altering agent behaviors using natural language instructions. *Proceedings of Autonomous Agents 2000.*

Bindiganavale, Rama, (2000). *Building parameterized action representations from observation*, Dissertation, University of Pennsylvania.

Chen, L., Hoey, J., Nugent, C. D., Cook, D. J., & Yu, Z. (2012a). Sensor-based activity recognition. *IEEE Transactions on Systems, Man, and Cybernetics*, 42(6), 790-808.

Chen, L., Nugent, C. D., & Wang, H. (2012b). A knowledge-driven approach to activity recognition in smart homes. *IEEE Transactions on Knowledge and Data Engineering, 24*(6), 961-974.

Deng, J., Dong, W., Socher, R., Li, L.J., Li, K. and Fei-Fei, L., 2009, June. Imagenet: A large-scale hierarchical image database. In *Computer Vision and Pattern Recognition, 2009. CVPR 2009. IEEE Conference on* (pp. 248-255). IEEE.

Doddington, G. R., Mitchell, A., Przybocki, M. A., Ramshaw, L. A., Strassel, S., & Weischedel, R. M. (2004, May). The Automatic Content Extraction (ACE) Program-Tasks, Data, and Evaluation. In *LREC* (Vol. 2, p. 1).

Eckle-Kohler, J., McCrae, J., & Chiarcos, C. (2014). lemonUby-a large, interlinked, syntactically-rich resource for ontologies. *Semantic Web Journal, submitted. special issue on Multilingual Linked Open Data.*

Fei-Fei, L. and Perona, P., 2005, June. A bayesian hierarchical model for learning natural scene categories. In *Computer Vision and Pattern Recognition, 2005. CVPR 2005. IEEE Computer Society Conference on* (Vol. 2, pp. 524-531). IEEE.

Fellbaum, C. (Ed.) (1998.) *WordNet: An Electronic Lexical Database.* MIT Press.

Fillmore, C. J. (1976). Frame semantics and the nature of language*. *Annals of the New York Academy of Sciences, 280*(1), 20-32.

Fillmore, C. J., & Baker, C. F. (2001, June). Frame semantics for text understanding. In *Proceedings of WordNet and Other Lexical Resources Workshop, NAACL.*

Fillmore, Charles J., Christopher R. Johnson, and Miriam R.L. Petruck. (2002.) Background to FrameNet. *International Journal of Lexicography*, 16(3):235-250.

Gu, T., Wang, X. H., Pung, H. K., & Zhang, D. Q. (2004). An ontology-based context model in intelligent environments. In *Communication networks and distributed systems modeling and simulation conference*, 270-275.

Hastings, J., Ceusters, W., Smith, B., & Mulligan, K. (2011). The emotion ontology: enabling interdisciplinary research in the affective sciences. In*Modeling and Using Context* (pp. 119-123). Springer Berlin Heidelberg.

Hogenboom, F., Frasincar, F., Kaymak, U., De Jong, F.An overview of event extraction from text. Workshop on Detection, Representation, and Exploitation of Events in the Semantic Web (DeRiVE 2011) at Tenth International Semantic Web Conference (ISWC 2011).

Ikuta, R., Styler IV, W. F., Hamang, M., O'Gorman, T., & Palmer, M. (2014). Challenges of Adding Causation to Richer Event Descriptions. *ACL 2014*, 12.

Jiang, Y.G., Liu, J., Zamir, A.R., Laptev, I., Piccardi, M., Shah, M., & Sukthankar. (2013). R.: THUMOS challenge: action recognition with a large number of classes. http://crcv.ucf.edu/ICCV13-Action-Workshop/.

Karpathy, A., Joulin, A. and Li, F.F.F., 2014. Deep fragment embeddings for bidirectional image sentence mapping. In *Advances in neural information processing systems* (pp. 1889-1897).

Kipper, Karin, Anna Korhonen, Neville Ryant, and Martha Palmer. (2008.) A large-scale classification of English verbs. *Language Resources and Evaluation Journal*, 42: pp. 21– 40.

Levin, B. (1993). *English verb classes and alternations: A preliminary investigation*. University of Chicago press.

Li, W., Zhang, Z., & Liu, Z. (2010). Action recognition based on a bag of 3d points. In *Computer Vision and Pattern Recognition Workshops (CVPRW)*, 9-14.

Liu, Z., J. Araki, E.H. Hovy, and T. Mitamura. (2014). Supervised Within-Document Event Coreference using Information Propagation. *Proceedings of the LREC conference*. Reykjavik, Iceland.

Masolo, C., Borgo, S., Gangemi, A., Guarino, N., Oltramari, A., & Schneider, L. (2003). Dolce: a descriptive ontology for linguistic and cognitive engineering. *WonderWeb Project, Deliverable D, 17*.

Noy, N. F., Sintek, M., Decker, S., Crubézy, M., Fergerson, R. W., & Musen, M. A. (2001). Creating semantic web contents with protege-2000.*IEEE intelligent systems*, (2), 60-71.

Nuzzolese, A. G., Gangemi, A., & Presutti, V. (2011, June). Gathering lexical linked data and knowledge patterns from FrameNet. In *Proceedings of the sixth international conference on Knowledge capture* (pp. 41-48). ACM.

Pease, A., Niles, I., & Li, J. (2002, July). The suggested upper merged ontology: A large ontology for the semantic web and its applications. In*Working notes of the AAAI-2002 workshop on ontologies and the semantic web* (Vol. 28).

Pustejovsky, J., Lee, K., Bunt, H. and Romary, L., (2010). ISO-TimeML: An International Standard for Semantic Annotation. In *LREC*.

Reed, S. L., & Lenat, D. B. (2002, July). Mapping ontologies into Cyc. In*AAAI 2002 Conference Workshop on Ontologies For The Semantic Web* (pp. 1-6).

Riboni, D., & Bettini, C. (2009). Context-aware activity recognition through a combination of ontological and statistical reasoning. In *Ubiquitous Intelligence and Computing*, 39-53.

Scheffczyk, J., Baker, C. F., & Narayanan, S. (2006). Ontology-based reasoning about lexical resources. In *Proc. of OntoLex* (pp. 1-8).

Smith, B., & Grenon, P. (2002). Basic formal ontology. *Draft. Downloadable at http://ontology. buffalo. edu/bfo*.

Song, Z., Bies, A., Strassel, S., Riese, T., Mott, J., Ellis, J., ... & Ma, X. (2015, June). From light to rich ERE: annotation of entities, relations, and events. In *Proceedings of the 3rd Workshop on EVENTS at the NAACL-HLT*(pp. 89-98.

Styler, William, F., Steven Bethard, Sean Finan, Martha Palmer, Sameer Pradhan, Piet C de Groen, Brad Erickson, Timothy Miller, Chen Lin, Guergana Savova and James Pustejovsky. (2014). Temporal Annotation in the Clinical Domain. *Transactions of the Association of Computational Linguistics*, 2, pp. 143-154.

Tahmoush, D. (2015). Applying Action Attribute Class Validation to Improve Human Activity Recognition. In *Proceedings of the IEEE Conference on Computer Vision and Pattern Recognition Workshops* (pp. 15-21).

Ye, J., Dobson, S., & McKeever, S. (2012). Situation identification techniques in pervasive computing: A review. *Pervasive and mobile computing*, *8*(1), 36-66.

A Comparison of Event Representations in DEFT

Ann Bies[a], Zhiyi Song[a], Jeremy Getman[a], Joe Ellis[a], Justin Mott[a], Stephanie Strassel[a], Martha Palmer[b], Teruko Mitamura[c], Marjorie Freedman[d], Heng Ji[e], Tim O'Gorman[b]

[a] Linguistic Data Consortium, University of Pennsylvania
3600 Market Street, Suite 810, Philadelphia, PA 19104, USA
{bies,zhiyi,jgetman,joellis,jmott,strassel}@ldc.upenn.edu
[b] University of Colorado at Boulder, Department of Linguistics
295 UCB, Boulder, CO 80309, USA
{Martha.Palmer,ogormant}@colorado.edu
[c] Language Technologies Institute, Carnegie Mellon University
6711 Gates-Hillman Center, 5000 Forbes Avenue, Pittsburgh, PA 15213, USA
teruko+@cs.cmu.edu
[d] Raytheon BBN Technologies
10 Moulton St., Cambridge, MA 02138, USA
mfreedma@bbn.com
[e] Rensselaer Polytechnic Institute, Department of Computer Science
110 8th Street, Troy, NY 12180, USA
jih@rpi.edu

Abstract

This paper will discuss and compare event representations across a variety of types of event annotation: Rich Entities, Relations, and Events (Rich ERE), Light Entities, Relations, and Events (Light ERE), Event Nugget (EN), Event Argument Extraction (EAE), Richer Event Descriptions (RED), and Event-Event Relations (EER). Comparisons of event representations are presented, along with a comparison of data annotated according to each event representation. An event annotation experiment is also discussed, including annotation for all of these representations on the same set of sample data, with the purpose of being able to compare actual annotation across all of these approaches as directly as possible. We walk through a brief example to illustrate the various annotation approaches, and to show the intersections among the various annotated data sets.

1 Introduction

This paper will discuss and compare event representations across the various types of event annotation that are part of the Deep Exploration and Filtering of Text (DEFT) program: Rich Entities, Relations, and Events (Rich ERE), Light Entities, Relations, and Events (Light ERE), Event Nugget (EN), Event Argument Extraction (EAE), Richer Event Descriptions (RED), and Event-Event Relations (EER). The DEFT program seeks to improve state-of-the-art capabilities in automated deep natural language processing, with a particular focus on technologies dealing with inference, causal relationships, and anomaly detection across several languages (DARPA, 2012). The processing of events and event-event relations underlies this focus. The annotation of events and event-event relations is a crucial part of supporting work on these technologies, and a variety of approaches are currently underway.

This paper presents a comparison of event representations, the data annotated, and possible future plans for event annotation. An event annota-

Proceedings of the 4th Workshop on Events: Definition, Detection, Coreference, and Representation, pages 27–36,
San Diego, California, June 17, 2016.

tion experiment is also discussed, in which the same set of sample data was annotated in each of the above representations, with the purpose of being able to compare actual annotation across all of these approaches as directly as possible. The paper walks through a brief example to illustrate the various annotation approaches, and to show the intersections among the various annotated data sets.

2 Types of Event Annotation in the DEFT Program

2.1 Entities, Relations, and Events (ERE)

ERE was developed as an annotation task that would be supportive of multiple research directions and evaluations in the DEFT program, and that would provide a useful foundation for more specialized annotation tasks like inference and anomaly. The ERE tasks include the annotation of entities, relations, and events and their attributes, according to a specific taxonomy, as was also done in Automatic Content Extraction (ACE) (LDC, 2005; Walker et al., 2006).

Light ERE was designed as a lighter-weight version of ACE and a simple approach to entity, relation, and event annotation, with the goal of making annotation easier and more consistent. Light ERE captures a reduced inventory of entity and relation types, with fewer attributes (compared to ACE; for example, only specific entities and actual relations are taggable, and entity subtypes are not labeled). The event ontology of Light ERE is similar to ACE, with slight modification and reduction, and there is strict coreference of events within documents (Aguilar et al., 2014). As in ACE, the annotation of each event mention includes the identification of a trigger, the labeling of the event type, subtype, and participating event argument entities and time expressions. Simplifying from ACE, only attested actual events are annotated (no irrealis events or arguments).

Rich ERE annotation expands on both the inventories and taggability of Light ERE (Song et al., 2015). Rich ERE Entity annotation adds non-specific entities and nominal head marking, in addition to adding a distinction between Location and Facility entity types. Rich ERE Relation annotation doubles the Light ERE ontology to twenty relation subtypes, and also adds future, hypothetical, and conditional relations. A new category of argument fillers was added for Rich ERE, to allow arguments that are not taggable as entities to be used as fillers for specific relation and event subtypes. For each event mention, Rich ERE labels the event type and subtype, its realis attribute, any of its arguments or participants that are present, and a required "trigger" string in the text. Rich ERE Event annotation includes increased taggability in several areas, compared to Light ERE or ACE event annotation: a slightly expanded event ontology, the addition of generic and other (irrealis) event mentions, the addition of event argument fillers that are otherwise not captured as entities, such as weapon, vehicle, money etc., the addition of argumentless triggers for event mentions, additional attributes for contact and transaction events, double tagging of event mentions for multiple types/subtypes, and multiple tagging of event mentions for certain types of coordination.

In Rich ERE, the concept of Event Hopper was also introduced as a more inclusive, less strict notion of event coreference than that used in Light ERE or ACE. Event hoppers contain mentions of events that are intuitively coreferential to the annotator even if they do not meet the earlier strict event identity requirement, and therefore group events according to a more inclusive coreference specification, which will allow a wider range of event mentions to be coreferential (Song et al., 2015). Event mentions could be placed into the same event hoppers even if they differed in temporal or trigger granularity, their arguments were non-coreferential or conflicting, or if their realis mood differed, as long as they referred to the same event with the same type and subtype. For example, in the following two sentences:

- *The White House didn't confirm Obama's* ***trip*** ***{Movement.TransportPerson, Other}*** *to Paris for the Climate Summit last year.*
- *Obama* ***went*** ***{Movement.Transport-Person, Actual}*** *to Paris for the Climate Summit.*

Although the realis label differs for the two mentions (Other vs. Actual), if both mentions refer to the same trip to Paris in the document context, they still belong to the same event hopper.

The development of Rich ERE is intended to lay the groundwork for upcoming expansion into the realm of event-event relations, as well as cross-document and even cross-lingual event representation.

2.2 Event Argument Extraction (EAE) and Event Argument Linking (EAL)

EAE was developed as a track within NIST's 2014 TAC Knowledge Base Population (KBP) (http://www.nist.gov/tac/) evaluation (Freedman et al., 2014). Following the paradigm of Slot Filling and Cold Start, two other KBP evaluation tracks, EAE in 2014 was evaluated by assessment over a pool of participant submissions (Ellis et al., 2014).

A KBP EAE submission consisted of a table of event arguments. For each argument, systems returned the event type/subtype, the argument's role in the event, a canonical mention of the argument entity (e.g., the most informative name string found for entity), textual justification of the extraction, a realis label (Actual, Generic, Other), and a confidence score. In the 2014 evaluation, the final pool of responses for scoring included a human-produced "manual run" developed by annotators along with up to 5 runs per participating team.

During assessment, annotators judged the correctness of the provided event type, the argument's assigned role in the event, the (possibly normalized) mention string of the argument entity, and the mention string for the argument entity from the larger provenance connecting it to the event. For correct responses, assessors also provided a realis label (Actual, Generic, Other), a mention type label (Name, Nominal, Other), and created equivalence class clusters. Assessment was performed on responses taken from approximately 250 source documents in 2014, 50 of which were dually assessed.

For dually assessed documents, agreement and kappa were calculated for two conditions (a) over all appropriate tags, (b) collapsing CORRECT and INEXACT (this reflects what is done for the official score). The agreement/kappa numbers only reflect cases where both annotators made an assessment (in some cases, e.g., assessors disagreed on the presence of event type – one assessor would perform an assessment and the other would not).

Numbers before the '/' are over all labels (requiring exact match); numbers after '/' collapse CORRECT and INEXACT. In official scoring, an answer is added to the GS if Realis matches and all of the following are CORRECT/INEXACT: AET, AER, BF, CAS. CAS Type is used for analyzing output, but is not a part of the scoring process.

AET (Event Presence)
    Agreement: 83.92% / 87.54%
    Agreement kappa: 64.41 / 69.55
AER (Event Role Presence)
    Agreement: 89.75% / 91.16%
    Agreement kappa: 58.42 / 61.18
BF (Base Filler)
    Agreement: 79.67% / 91.08%
    Agreement kappa: 65.54 / 74.52
CAS
    Agreement: 76.89% / 84.26%
    Agreement kappa: 64.28 / 67.19
CAS Type
    Agreement: 80.50%
    Agreement kappa: 57.26
Realis
    Agreement: 87.18%
    Agreement kappa: 61.90

The EAE task (and assessed results) differs in three important ways from the Rich ERE annotation. (1) The EAE task is assessed at the level of 'entity' and 'document-level-event' and not at the level of the event mention. As such, a system need only find an argument one time, even when an entity's participation in some event is made explicit in several mentions throughout a document. (2) The EAE task treats as correct a broader set inference about arguments, for example inferring the date/location of an event through general reasoning over the document or inferring participation in an event through group membership. (3) The EAE task does not assess a sub-sentence linguistic trigger/justification of the event. Instead the event type (ET) assessment of EAE task assesses whether or not a sentence length unit justifies the event given a reasonable reader's interpretation.

In 2015, EAE was extended to require systems to group together arguments participating in the same event. In the updated version of the task, named Event Argument Linking (EAL) and conducted as part of the 2015 TAC KBP evaluations, event arguments were extracted following the same guidelines as EAE, but then had to be grouped together into Event Hoppers, as defined by the Rich ERE task. Performance was measured by comparing system-developed argument clusters against those created by annotators following assessment, which included all responses provided by systems for each document (Ellis et al., 2015).

To support the 2015 linking task, correct, non-generic assessments from the system submitted output were grouped into argument-sets of hopper-sized granularity. This annotation was performed on 50 sample documents as development data for the 2015 EAL evaluation and on 81 documents in the 2015 EAL test set. The development data overlaps with data for which Rich ERE annotation was performed. The overlapping data set could be used to explore how the differences in annotation procedure lead to differences in decisions about event granularity.

2.3 Event Nugget (EN)

An Event Nugget is a tuple of an event trigger, classification of event type and subtype, and realis attribute. It is similar to an event mention in ERE, but arguments are not labelled. EN annotation in 2014 focused on event nuggets (expanded triggers) only, and followed the same taxonomy of 33 event types and subtypes as Light ERE. However, instead of tagging minimal extent as the trigger, EN allowed multi-word event nuggets (Mitamura et al., 2015). Multi-word event nuggets can be either continuous or discontinuous, and are based on the goal of marking the maximal extent of a semantically meaningful unit to express the event in a sentence. EN also added a realis attribute for each event mention. The realis attribute labels each event as Actual, Generic, or Other. TAC KBP 2014 conducted a pilot evaluation on Event Nugget Detection (END), in which systems were required to detect event nugget tuples, consisting of an event trigger, the type and subtype classification, and the realis attribute.

Relation Type	Inheritance	Expansion	Contingency	Comparison	Temporality
Subtype (sense)	Reemergence Sub-event Variation Coreference	Confirmation Conjunction Disjunction	Condition Causality	Competition Concession Negation Opposite	Before-After Start Vagueness Meet Overlap During Equality Finish

Table 1: EER event relation types.

In 2015, TAC KBP ran an open evaluation on EN that was expanded to three evaluation tasks: Event Nugget Detection, Event Nugget Detection and Coreference, and Event Nugget Coreference. Full Event Nugget Coreference is identified when two or more Event Nuggets refer to the same event. EN annotation in 2015 followed the Rich ERE event taxonomy, which added 5 event types and subtypes to make a total of 38 event types and subtypes, and also followed the Rich ERE guidelines on trigger extents, which adopted the minimal extent rule and disallowed discontinuous event triggers (Song et al., 2016). Annotation of Event Nugget Coreference adopted the concept of Event Hopper as in Rich ERE.

2.4 Event-Event Relations (EER)

EER annotation focuses on relations between events in the ERE/ACE taxonomy, both within document and cross-document (Hong et al., 2016). Our general goal is to construct event-centric knowledge networks, where each node is an event and the edges effectively capture the relations between any two events. EER includes five main types of event relations – Inheritance, Expansion, Contingency, Comparison and Temporality – along with 21 sense-based subtypes (or relation senses), as shown in Table 1.

Events involved in a relation play certain roles. For example, an Attack event and an Injure event in a Contingency_Causality will play Cause and Result roles respectively. Figure 1 shows more information about types and roles.

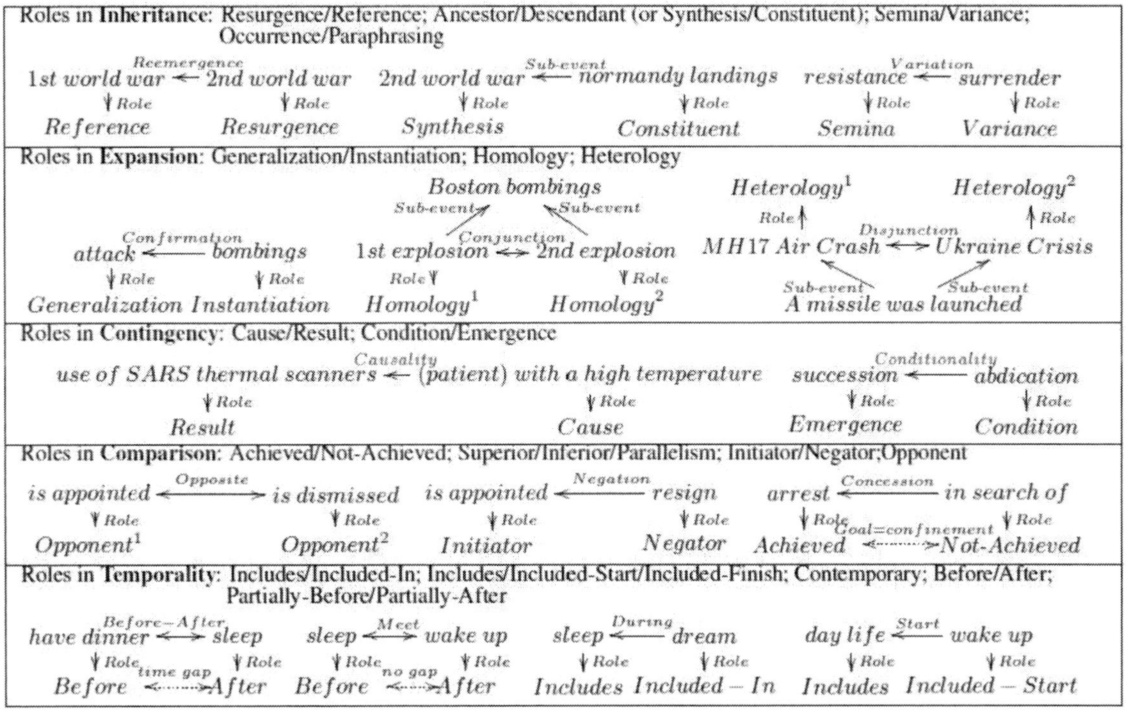

Figure 1: Roles and examples specific to fine-grained event-event relation subtypes.

2.5 Richer Event Descriptions (RED)

RED annotation (Ikuta et al., 2014) marks all events in a document, as well as certain relations between those events. RED combines coreference (Pradhan et al., 2007; Lee et al., 2012) and THYME Temporal Relations annotation (Styler et al., 2014) to provide a thorough representation of entities, events and their relations. The RED schema also goes beyond prior annotations of coreference or temporal relations by also annotating subevent structure, cause-effect relations and reporting relations. Guidelines for RED annotation can be found at https://github.com/timjogorman/RicherEventDescription/blob/master/guidelines.md.

3 Annotation Features and Data Annotated

The representation of events and the scope of annotation vary across the different annotation approaches. Table 2 compares the definition of events in each annotation. Table 3 compares how event coreference and event relations are annotated. Table 4 shows the annotated data volume for each annotation schema, completed as of 2015. Annotated data has been distributed to DEFT performers, and will be made available to the wider community as part of the Linguistic Data Consortium (LDC) catalog.

	Event Type and Subtype	Modality/Realis	Arguments	Trigger
Light ERE	8 types 33 subtypes	Actual	Labelled, must include at least one	Minimal span
Rich ERE	9 types 38 subtypes	Actual, Generic, Other	Labelled, but events with no arguments are possible	Minimal span
Event Argument 2014 – 2015	9 types 31 subtypes	Actual, Generic, Other	At least one	Event mentions are not tagged
Event Nugget 2014	8 types 33 subtypes	Actual, Generic, Other	No	Maximal semantic unit
Event Nugget 2015	9 types 38 subtypes	Actual, Generic, Other	No	Minimal span
Event-event relation	8 types 33 subtypes	Actual, Generic, Other	No	Minimal span
RED	Untyped, all predicating events	Actual, Generic, Hypothetical, Uncertain/hedged	No	Single word

Table 2: What is a taggable event mention in each representation.

	Identity coreference	Event-event relations
Light ERE	Strict identity	n/a
Rich ERE	Hopper	n/a
Event Argument 2014	n/a	n/a
Event Argument 2015	Hopper	n/a
Event Nugget 2015	Hopper	n/a
Event-event relation	Strict identity	5 types 21 subtypes
RED	Strict identity, Narrative Containers, Subevent, Set/Member	Aspectual, Causation, Reporting, Temporal

Table 3: Event-event relations in each representation.

	Event Experiment	2014	2015
Rich ERE	52 docs	--	English: 375Kw Chinese:245Kw Spanish: 139Kw
Event Argument	55 docs	519 docs	300 docs
Event Nugget	55 docs	English: 470Kw	English: 210K words
Event-event relation	11 docs	60 docs	79 documents (343 events, 20,235 pairs, 594 related pairs)
RED	55 docs	20 docs	100 docs

Table 4: Volume of data manually annotated for the Event Experiment, for 2014, and for 2015.

4 Comparison: The Event Annotation Experiment

As a result of this diversity in event annotation within DEFT, the Event Working Group which is focusing on events within DEFT has initiated an experiment in which participating teams perform event annotations on the same set of data using all of the different annotation schemas. The goal of the experiment is to make the differences and similarities between the approaches more apparent and to facilitate comparison.

The 50 documents that had been dually assessed for EAE in 2014 were chosen as the data set for the experiment, as both system output and human assessment already exists for the data. Additionally, five newswire documents from the EAE pilot data pool were identified as particularly challenging for event annotation, and so these five documents were also included in the experiment set.

The annotation for this experiment has been completed and released to the DEFT community (LDC, 2015) and will be subsequently published in LDC's catalog, making it available to the broader research community. EN annotation in this experiment adopted the 2014 annotation schema, instead of the 2015 schema. Additionally EAE annotation in the experiment did not group arguments of the same event.

To illustrate the differences of the annotation tasks, below are the annotations in each representation for the following two sentences:

Media tycoon Barry Diller on Wednesday quit as chief of Vivendi Universal Entertainment. Parent company chairman Jean-Rene Fourtou will replace Diller as chief executive of US unit.

Rich ERE, **Light ERE**, **EN**, and **EAE**: Shown in Table 5.

1. Hopper	2. Trigger	3. Type.Subtype	4. Realis	5. Arguments
Hopper 1	*quit*	Personnel.EndPosition	Actual	*Barry Diller* *chief* *Wednesday*
	replace		Actual	*Diller* *Chief*
Hopper 2	*replace*	Personnel.StartPosition	Other	*Jean-Rene Fourtou* *Chief*

Table 5: Event annotation experiment example annotation for Rich ERE (the full table), Light ERE (Hopper 1 only, columns 1-3, 5), EN (columns 1-4), and EAE (columns 1, 3-5).

RED: There are two events in the sentence according to RED. The first predicate, *quit*, is tagged as an Actual Event that occurs BEFORE Document Time. The second, *replace*, is tagged as an Actual Event that is expected to occur AFTER Document Time. RED also labels a causal and temporal relation between the two events, "BEFORE/PRECONDITIONS", showing that the quitting event leads to, but does not directly cause, the replacement, and a temporal CONTAINS relation linking *quit* to Wednesday.

- Event 1: *quit* - BEFORE DOCTIME, Actual Modality
- Event 2: *replace* - AFTER DOCTIME, Actual Modality
- Relation 1: *quit* BEFORE/ PRECONDITIONS *replace*
- Relation 2: *Wednesday* CONTAINS *quit*

Although RED does not annotate the arguments of events, it is intended to be combined with semantic role annotations such as PropBank (Bonial et al., 2014) or AMR (Banarescu et al., 2013), which would provide the argument information. For this example, the *quit* and *replace* events would also be given the predicate argument structures below:

quit.01
    Arg0: Media Tycoon Barry Diller
    Arg1: as chief of Vivendi Universal Entertainment
    ArgM-TMP: on Wednesday

replace.01
    Arg2: Parent company chairman Jean-Rene Fourtou
    Arg1: Diller
    ArgM-MOD: will
    ArgM-PRD: as chief executive of US unit.

EER: The following events are connected by *Condition* and *Temporality* relations:

- Event 1 (Personnel.EndPosition): *quit*
- Event 2 (Personnel.StartPosition): *replace*

A preliminary analysis of the Rich ERE and Event Argument annotations shows that EAE includes more annotated events, since both non-inferred and inferred events are targeted by EAE, while Rich ERE currently does not annotate inferred events. Initial analysis of Rich ERE and Event Nugget annotation shows that there is considerable overlap in event mentions annotated in both Rich ERE and EN 2014. The main differences are as expected due to the differences in the annotation tasks, namely (1) annotated extents (EN 2014 tags maximal extents of event nuggets to capture the complete semantic unit of the nugget, whereas Rich ERE captures the minimal extent of the event trigger), and (2) double tagging (Rich ERE allows annotation of the same event trigger more than once when the trigger instantiates more than one event type/subtype or in case of conjunction, while EN in 2014 annotated each nugget for a single event type/subtype). To better align with the EAE evaluation as well as the existing Rich ERE annotated data, EN 2015 adopted the Rich ERE guidelines so these differences between Rich ERE and EN 2014 were eliminated.

5 Future Work

In future and on-going work, several of these approaches are coming together in certain aspects for the purpose of conducting event evaluations.

To avoid producing different annotation datasets to support Event Argument and Event Nugget evaluation (as was the case in both 2014 and 2015) and to bring Event Argument and Event Nugget evaluation together to address the goals of extraction and clustering of events for populating a knowledge base, both Event Argument and Event Nugget will use Event annotation in Rich ERE as evaluation data in 2016. Event Argument will be switching to a gold-standard based evaluation for measuring performance in extracting event arguments and within-document grouping of arguments when they participate in the same event. Event Nugget will evaluate event nugget detection and coreference, as in 2015. Both Event Argument and Event Nugget evaluations will be expanded to multiple languages (English, Chinese and Spanish). For both, the set of valid event types will be reduced to the 18 listed below:

```
Conflict.Attack
Conflict.Demonstrate
Contact.Broadcast
Contact.Contact
Contact.Correspondence
Contact.Meet
Justice.Arrest-Jail
Life.Die
Life.Injure
Manufacture.Artifact
Movement.TransportArtifact
Movement.TransportPerson
Personnel.Elect
Personnel.EndPosition
Personnel.StartPosition
Transaction.Transaction
Transaction.TransferMoney
Transaction.TransferOwnership
```

Additionally, a query- and assessment-based evaluation will also be conducted as a task in Event Argument evaluation to test capabilities in cross-document clustering of events. The size of the evaluation source corpus for Event Argument will increase dramatically (from 500 documents in 2015 to 90,000 documents in 2016).

Finally, the EN team is working on a possible pilot evaluation for 'event sequencing' for 2016.

6 Conclusion

The variety of event representations and annotations in the DEFT program seek to tackle the issues of event annotation from multiple directions, and each type of representation brings an aspect of the larger event picture into focus. The comparisons across these representations that will be possible using the annotation from the Event Annotation Experiment will provide on-going useful information as event annotation evolves to meet the goals of the DEFT program and the research community.

Acknowledgments

This material is based on research sponsored by Air Force Research Laboratory and Defense Advanced Research Projects Agency under agreement number FA8750-13-2-0045. The U.S. Government is authorized to reproduce and distribute reprints for Governmental purposes notwithstanding any copyright notation thereon. The views and conclusions contained herein are those of the authors and should not be interpreted as necessarily representing the official policies or endorsements, either expressed or implied, of Air Force Research Laboratory and Defense Advanced Research Projects Agency or the U.S. Government.

References

Jacqueline Aguilar, Charley Beller, Paul McNamee, Benjamin Van Durme, Stephanie Strassel, Zhiyi Song, Joe Ellis. 2014. A Comparison of the Events and Relations Across ACE, ERE, TAC-KBP, and FrameNet Annotation Standards. ACL 2014: 52nd Annual Meeting of the Association for Computational Linguistics, Baltimore, June 22-27. *2nd Workshop on Events: Definition, Detection, Coreference, and Representation*.

L. Banarescu, C. Bonial, S. Cai, M. Georgescu, K. Griffitt, U. Hermjakob, K. Knight, P. Koehn, M. Palmer, and N. Schneider. 2013. Abstract Meaning Representation for Sembanking. *Proc. Linguistic Annotation Workshop*.

Claire Bonial, Julia Bonn, Kathryn Conger, Jena Hwang and Martha Palmer. 2014. PropBank: Semantics of New Predicate Types. *The 9th edition of the Language Resources and Evaluation Conference*. Reykjavik, Iceland.

DARPA. 2012. *Broad Agency Announcement: Deep Exploration and Filtering of Text (DEFT)*. Defense Advanced Research Projects Agency, DARPA-BAA-12-47.

Joe Ellis, Jeremy Getman, Dana Fore, Neil Kuster, Zhiyi Song, Ann Bies, Stephanie Strassel. 2015. Overview of Linguistic Resources for the TAC KBP 2015 Evaluations: Methodologies and Results. In *Proceedings of TAC KBP 2015 Workshop, National Institute of Standards and Technology*, Gaithersburg, Maryland, USA, November 16-17, 2015.

Joe Ellis, Jeremy Getman, Stephanie M. Strassel. 2014. Overview of Linguistic Resources for the TAC KBP 2014 Evaluations: Planning, Execution, and Results. In *Proceedings of TAC KBP 2014 Workshop, National Institute of Standards and Technology*, Gaithersburg, Maryland, USA, November 17-18, 2014.

Marjorie Freedman and Ryan Gabbard. 2014. Overview of the Event Argument Evaluation. In *Proceedings of TAC KBP 2014 Workshop, National Institute of Standards and Technology*, Gaithersburg, Maryland, USA, November 17-18, 2014.

Yu Hong, Tongtao Zhang, Sharone Horowit-Hendler, Heng Ji, Tim O'Gorman and Martha Palmer. 2016. Building a Cross-document Event-Event Relation Corpus. Submitted.

Rei Ikuta, William F. Styler IV, Mariah Hamang, Tim O'Gorman, and Martha Palmer, 2014. Challenges of Adding Causation to Richer Event Descriptions. In *Proceedings of the 2nd Workshop on EVENTS: Definition, Detection, Coreference, and Representation*, pages 12–20, Baltimore, Maryland, USA, June 22-27, 2014. © 2014 Association for Computational Linguistics.

H. Lee, M. Recasens, A. Chang, M. Surdeanu, and D. Jurafsky. 2012. Joint entity and event coreference resolution across documents. In *Proceedings of the Conference on Empirical Methods in Natural Language Processing and Computational Natural Language Learning* (EMNLP-CoNLL), Jeju Island, 489-500.

Linguistic Data Consortium. 2005. *ACE (Automatic Content Extraction) English Annotation Guidelines for Events Version 5.4.3.*

Linguistic Data Consortium. 2015. *DEFT Event Annotation Comparison Experiment V1.* Catalog ID: LDC2015E40, Linguistic Data Consortium.

Teruko Mitamura, Yukari Yamakawa, Sue Holm, Zhiyi Song, Ann Bies, Seth Kulick, Stephanie Strassel. 2015. Event Nugget Annotation: Processes and Issues. The 2015 Conference of the North American Chapter of the Association for Computational Linguistics - Human Language Technologies (NAACL HLT 2015). *3rd Workshop on EVENTS: Definition, Detection, Coreference, and Representation.*

S. Pradhan, L. Ramshaw, R. Weischedel, J. MacBride, and L. Micciulla. 2007. Unrestricted Coreference: Indentifying Entities and Events in OntoNotes. In *Proceedings of the IEEE International Conference on Semantic Computing* (ICSC), September 17-19.

Zhiyi Song, Ann Bies, Stephanie Strassel, Tom Riese, Justin Mott, Joe Ellis, Jonathan Wright, Seth Kulick, Neville Ryant and Xiaoyi Ma. 2015. From Light to Rich ERE: Annotation of Entities, Relations, and Events. The 2015 Conference of the North American Chapter of the Association for Computational Linguistics - Human Language Technologies (NAACL HLT 2015). *3rd Workshop on EVENTS: Definition, Detection, Coreference, and Representation.*

Zhiyi Song, Ann Bies, Stephanie Strassel, Joe Ellis, Teruko Mitamura, Hoa Dong, Yukari Yamakawa, Sue Holm. 2016. Event Nugget and Event Coreference Annotation. The 2016 Conference of the North American Chapter of the Association for Computational Linguistics - Human Language Technologies (NAACL HLT 2016). *4th Workshop on EVENTS: Definition, Detection, Coreference, and Representation.*

W. F. Styler, S. Bethard, S. Finan, M. Palmer, S. Pradhan, P. C. de Groen, B. Erickson, T. Miller, C. Lin, G. Savova and J. Pustejovsky. 2014. Temporal Annotation in the Clinical Domain, *Transactions of the Association of Computational Linguistics*, 2:143–154.

Christopher Walker, Stephanie Strassel, Julie Medero, Kazuaki Maeda. 2006. *ACE 2005 Multilingual Training Corpus*. Linguistic Data Consortium, LDC Catalog No.: LDC2006T06.

Event Nugget and Event Coreference Annotation

Zhiyi Song[a], Ann Bies[a], Stephanie Strassel[a], Joe Ellis[a], Teruko Mitamura[b], Hoa Dang[c], Yukari Yamakawa[b], Sue Holm[b]

[a]Linguistic Data Consortium, University of Pennsylvania,
3600 Market Street, suite 810, Philadelphia, PA 19104, USA
{zhiyi, bies, strassel, joellis}@ldc.upenn.edu
[b]Language Technologies Institute, Carnegie Mellon University,
6711 Gates-Hillman Center, 5000 Forbes Ave., Pittsburgh, PA 15213, USA
teruko+@cs.cmu.edu, yukariy@andrew.cmu.edu, sh4s@andrew.cmu.edu
[c]National Institute of Standards and Technology, 100 Bureau Drive, Gaithersburg, MD 20899, USA
hoa.dang@nist.gov

Abstract

In this paper, we describe the event nugget annotation created in support of the pilot Event Nugget Detection evaluation in 2014 and in support of the Event Nugget Detection and Coreference open evaluation in 2015, which was one of the Knowledge Base Population tracks within the NIST Text Analysis Conference. We present the data volume annotated for both training and evaluation data for the 2015 evaluation as well as changes to annotation in 2015 as compared to that of 2014. We also analyze the annotation for the 2015 evaluation as an example to show the annotation challenges and consistency, and identify the event types and subtypes that are most difficult for human annotators. Finally, we discuss annotation issues that we need to take into consideration in the future.

1 Introduction

The Text Analysis Conference (TAC) is a series of workshops organized by the National Institute of Standards and Technology (NIST), aiming to encourage research in natural language processing (NLP). The Knowledge Base Population (KBP) tracks of TAC encourage the development of systems that can match entities mentioned in natural texts with those appearing in a knowledge base and extract information about entities from a document collection and add it to a new or existing knowledge base. Starting in 2014, TAC KBP added a track for event evaluation. The goal of the TAC KBP Event track is to extract information about events such that the information would be suitable as input to a knowledge base.

Event Nugget (EN) evaluation, as one of the evaluation tasks in the TAC KBP event track, aims to evaluate system performance on EN detection and EN coreference (Mitamura & Hovy, 2015). An event nugget, as defined by the task, includes a text extent that instantiates an event, a classification of event type and subtype, and an indication of the realis of the event. This is different from nuggets (Voorhees, 2003; Babko-Malaya, et al, 2012) and the Summary Content Units (SCU) described in (Nenkova and Passnoneau, 2004; Nenkova et al, 2007) where nuggets and SCU are units of meaning (usually in the form of a sentential clause) which not only includes the main verb/word that instantiates an event, but also all arguments.

In this paper, we describe the event nugget annotation to support the pilot EN Detection evaluation

Proceedings of the 4th Workshop on Events: Definition, Detection, Coreference, and Representation, pages 37–45, San Diego, California, June 17, 2016.

in 2014 and in support of the EN Detection and Coreference TAC KBP open evaluation in 2015. We discuss changes to the annotation in 2015 as compared to that of 2014 and present the data volume annotated for both training and evaluation data for the 2015 evaluation. We analyze the annotation for the 2015 evaluation data to show the annotation and consistency challenges, identify the event types and subtypes that are most difficult for human annotators, and finally discuss annotation issues that we need to take into consideration in the future.

2 Event Nugget Evaluation in TAC KBP

The EN evaluation was introduced in 2014 and run as a pilot evaluation, which sought to serve two purposes. One was to measure event detection by performers' systems in the Deep Exploration and Filtering of Text (DEFT) program of the Defense Advanced Research Projects Agency (DARPA, 2012). The program aims to address remaining capability gaps in state-of-the-art natural language processing technologies related to inference, causal relationships and anomaly detection. The other purpose of the pilot, however, was to test run the evaluation framework before opening it up to the full TAC KBP community. The Pilot EN evaluation had one evaluation task:

- EN Detection: Participating systems must identify all relevant Event Mention instances in English texts, categorize each mention's Event types/subtype and identify its realis value (ACTUAL, GENERIC, or OTHER).

As the pilot was considered a success, EN was added to the roster of full-fledged evaluation tracks for TAC KBP 2015, with some modifications to incorporate lessons learned from the pilot and to better align with the other TAC KBP 2015 event-related evaluations – Event Argument Linking (EAL) (Freedman, 2014 & 2015) – and also the Entities, Relations and Events (ERE) data provided to KBP participants for training purposes. The EN evaluation in TAC KBP 2015 included two new tasks in addition to EN Detection:

- EN Detection and Coreference: Participating systems must identify not only the event nugget, but also full event coreference links. Full Event Coreference is identified when two or more event nuggets refer to the same event.
- EN Coreference: Participating systems must identify full event coreference links, given the annotated event nuggets in the text.

ERE was developed as an annotation task that would be supportive of multiple research directions and evaluations in the DEFT program, and that would provide a useful foundation for more specialized annotation tasks like inference and anomaly. The resulting ERE annotation task has evolved over the course of the program, from a fairly lightweight treatment of entities, relations and events in text (Light ERE), to a richer representation of phenomena of interest to the program (Rich ERE) (Song, et al., 2015). In ERE Event annotation, each event mention has annotation of event type and subtype, its realis attribute, any of its arguments or participants that are present, and a required "trigger" string in the text; furthermore, event mentions within the same document are coreferenced into event hoppers (Song, et al., 2015). EN annotation includes all of these annotations, except the annotation of event arguments.

The EN task in 2014 adapted the event annotation guidelines from the Light ERE annotation task (Aguilar, et al., 2014) by incorporating modifications by the evaluation coordinators that focused on the text extents establishing valid references to events, clarifications on transaction event types, and the additional annotation of event realis attributes, which indicated whether each event mention was asserted (Actual), generic or habitual (Generic), or some other category, such as future, hypothetical, negated, or uncertain (Other) (Mitamura, et al., 2015) .

In 2015, EN annotation followed the Rich ERE Event annotation guidelines (except for the annotation of event arguments). As compared to EN annotation in 2014, Rich ERE Event annotation and 2015 EN annotation include increased taggability in several areas: slightly expanded event ontology, additional attributes for contact and transaction events, and double tagging of event mentions for multiple types/subtypes and for certain types of coordination, in addition to event coreference.General Instructions

3 Event Nugget Annotation

In this section, we describe the EN annotation as well as the major differences between the 2014 and 2015 annotation tasks.

3.1 Event Trigger

An event trigger span is the textual extent within a sentence that indicates a reference to a valid event of a limited set of event types and subtypes. In the 2014 EN task, the trigger span was defined as a semantically meaningful unit which could be either a single word (main verb, noun, adjective, adverb) or a continuous or discontinuous multi-word phrase (Mitamura et al., 2015). For the 2015 EN evaluation, trigger span was redefined as the smallest, contiguous extent of text (usually a word or phrase) that most saliently expresses the occurrence of an event. This change brings consistency to the EN annotation of event trigger with approaches taken in Automatic Content Extraction (ACE) (LDC, 2005) as well as Light and Rich ERE (Song et al, 2015). Additionally, we see improved annotation consistency in terms of event trigger extent, as shown in Figure 1 of section 5.1. Unlike in the 2014 EN annotation, annotators for the 2015 data were allowed to 'double tag' event triggers in order to indicate that a given text extent referred to more than one event type/subtype, which was usually used to indicate the presence of an obligatorily inferred event. Double tagging was also used for certain types of coordination. For example, given the following text:

> *Cipriani was sentenced to life in prison for the **murder** of Renault chief George Besse in 1986 and the head of government arms sales Rene Audran a year earlier.*

In 2015 EN annotation, the word "murder" would be the trigger for two Life.Die events, one with the victim "George Besse" and the other with "Rene Audran" as well as two Conflict.Attack events, one occurring in 1986 and the other in 1985. In 2014 EN annotation, the word "murder" would be the trigger for only one Conflict.Attack event.

3.2 Event Taxonomy

EN annotation and evaluation focus on a limited inventory of event types and subtypes, as defined in ERE, based on Automatic Content Extraction (Doddington et al., 2004; Walker et al., 2006; Aguilar et al., 2014; Song et al., 2015). The 2014 EN evaluation covered the inventory of event types and subtypes from Light ERE, including 8 event types and 33 subtypes.

The 2015 evaluation added a new event type (Manufacture) and four new subtypes – Movement.TransportArtifact, Contact.Broadcast, Contact.Contact, Transaction.Transaction – which aligned the EN event ontology with that of Rich ERE in order to take advantage of the existing Rich ERE annotated data as training data. The EN annotation task also adopted a new approach for applying the Contact event subtype categorizations, which had been developed for Rich ERE data creation efforts. Instead of having annotators categorize the subtypes directly, Contact event mentions were labeled with attributes to describe formality (Formal, Informal, Can't Tell), scheduling (Planned, Spontaneous, Can't Tell), medium (In-person, Not-in-person, Can't Tell), and audience (Two-way, One-way, Can't Tell). Contact event subtypes were automatically generated based on the annotated attributes. This change added increased granularity to the Contact events and captured more subtypes, which had been requested by data users, and it also allowed the annotation to provide information at two levels, the attribute level and the traditional event subtype level, which may support more robust system development.

3.3 Event Coreference

The final change to the 2015 EN evaluation as compared to the 2014 pilot was the added requirement of event coreference. Again following the Rich ERE task, EN annotation in 2015 adopted the notion of 'event hoppers', a more inclusive, less strict notion of event coreference as compared to previous approaches as in ACE (LDC, 2005) and Light ERE. The notion of event hopper was introduced to address the pervasive challenges of event coreference, with respect to event mention and event argument granularity (Song, et al., 2015). Following this approach, event mentions were added to an event hopper when they were intuitively coreferential to an annotator, even if they did not meet a strict event identity requirement. Event nuggets could be placed into the same event hoppers even if they differed in temporal or trigger granularity, their arguments were non-coreferential or conflicting, or even if their realis mood differed, as long as they referred to the same event with the same type and subtype. For example, in the following two sentences:

- *The White House didn't confirm Obama's* ***trip*** ***{Movement.TransportPerson, Other}*** *to Paris for the Climate Summit last year.*
- *Obama* ***went*** ***{Movement.TransportPerson, Actual}*** *to Paris for the Climate Summit.*

The first event nugget's realis label is Other while the second event nugget is Actual. From the context, we know that both nuggets are talking about the same trip to Paris, so even though they have different realis labels, they still belong to the same event hopper.

4 Training and Evaluation Data

In this section, we present the training and evaluation data annotated to support the EN evaluation in 2015.

4.1 Training Data

Due to the changes in Rich ERE event annotation (and hence 2015 EN annotation) as compared to EN annotation in 2014, the 2014 evaluation data set was re-annotated so that the annotation matched the Rich ERE standard. Additionally Rich ERE annotation is created as a core resource for the DEFT program and TAC KBP evaluation, aiming to provide a valuable resource for multiple evaluations. Rich ERE annotation includes exhaustive annotation of Entities, Relations, Events and Event Hoppers, and 2015 EN annotation shares the Rich ERE annotation guidelines for Events, with the exception that Events and Event hoppers in Rich ERE also include the annotation of event arguments. Table 1 lists the total training data volume available for the 2015 EN evaluation.

Annotation	Genre	Files	Words	EN	Hoppers
EN and Coref	NW	81	27,897	2,219	1,461
EN and Coref	DF	77	97,124	4,319	1,874
Rich ERE	DF	240	156,041	4,192	3,044
Rich ERE	NW	48	23,999	1,571	1,099
Total		446	305,061	12,301	7,478

Table 1: Training Data Volume for 2015 Event Nugget.

4.2 Evaluation Data

Source data for the 2015 EN evaluation was a subset of the documents selected for EAL evaluation, which had been manually selected to ensure coverage of all event types and subtypes for that evaluation. Tokenization of the source documents was also provided. Unlike the 2014 data, in which annotation was performed on pre-tokenized text, in 2015 tokenization was performed as a post-annotation procedure, using tool kits provided by evaluation coordinators.

In order to reduce the impact of low recall on annotation consistency, which had proven problematic in the pilot and in previous event annotation efforts (Mitamura et al., 2015), gold standard EN data was produced by first having two annotators perform EN annotation (which included the creation of event hoppers) independently for each document (referred to as first pass 1 or FP1, and first pass 2 or FP2, below), which was followed by an adjudication pass conducted by a senior annotator to resolve disagreements and add annotation that was otherwise missed in one of the first passes. The EN annotation team consisted of nine annotators, six of whom were also adjudicators, and care was taken to ensure that annotators did not adjudicate their own files. Following adjudication of all documents, a corpus-wide quality control pass was also performed. In this pass, annotators manually scanned a list of all event triggers to review event type and subtype values and all event hoppers to make sure that event mentions in the same hopper have same type and subtype value. All identified outliers were then manually reviewed in context, and corrected if needed.

Annotation	Genre	Files	Words	EN	Hoppers
EN and Coref	NW	98	49,319	3,788	2,440
EN and Coref	DF	104	39,333	2,650	1,685
Total		202	88,652	6,438	4,125

Table 2: Evaluation Data Volume for 2015 Event Nugget.

The evaluation data set consists of 202 documents with a total word count of 88,652. The gold standard annotation has a total of 6,438 event nuggets and 4,125 event hoppers in total. Table 2 shows the profile of the evaluation dataset.

Appendix 1 shows the distribution of each type-subtype in the evaluation data. Conflict.Attack has the highest representation (591 event nuggets) while

Business.EndOrg has the lowest count (6). With the two newly added contact subtypes (Contact and Broadcast), there are altogether 1,491 contact event nuggets (23%), with 1,101 Contact.Contact and Contact.Broadcast combined (17%). Each event nugget is labeled with one of the three realis attributes: actual, generic and other. Table 3 shows the distribution of event nugget realis annotation by genres.

realis	NW	DF
actual	2,508	1,595
generic	603	539
other	677	516
total	3,788	2,650

Table 3: Event Nugget counts by realis attributes in NW and DF genres.

5 Inter-annotator Agreement and Annotation Challenges

Subsequent analysis of inter-annotator agreement in the EN 2015 evaluation data indicates that several challenges remain to be addressed.

5.1 Inter-annotator Agreement

Annotation consistency is generally in line with what we expect due to the complex nature of event recognition. The changes in the approach to the annotation task that were described above appear to have made some improvements, as shown in Figure 1, which compares the overall inter-annotator agreement (IAA) on first pass EN annotation in 2014 and 2015. Compared with 2014, IAA F1 score in 2015 improved by 5% in event trigger detection ("plain" in Figure 3) and realis attribute labelling. There is only 1% of improvement on event type and subtype classification. Regarding event coreference, which was new in 2015, the IAA F1 score was 67.63%. Below are a few examples indicating disagreement in event trigger, event typing and realis attributes:

Trigger extent mismatch:

- *She met the insurance investment magnate Shelby Cullom Davis on a* ***train*** *(FP1: Movement.TransportPerson)* ***to*** *(FP2: Movement.TransportPerson) Geneva in 1930.*

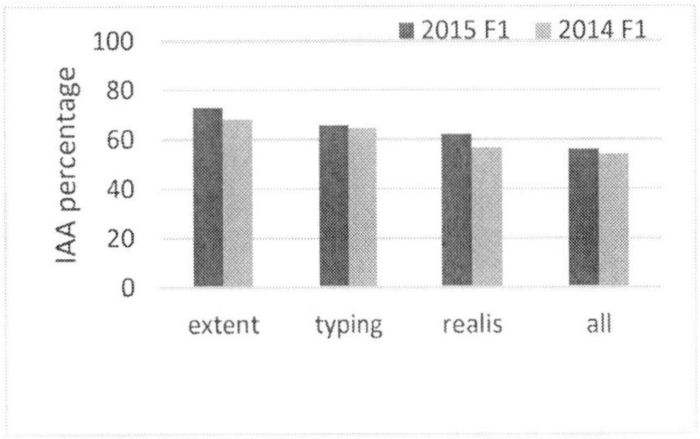

Figure 1: Inter-annotator agreement on first pass EN annotation in 2014 and 2015.

Mention type/subtype mismatch:

- *Dr. Yusuf Sonmez whom he called a notorious international organ* ***trafficker****. (FP1: Movement.TransportArtifact; FP2: Transaction.TransferOwnership)*

Realis Attribute mismatch:

- *The wealthy, ailing patients who were to* ***receive*** *(FP1: Actual; FP2: Other) the organs flew to Pristina.*

Some types scored better than others. As expected, Contact and Transaction event types have the lowest consistency. Figure 2 displays the IAA F1 scores on first pass EN annotation by event types.

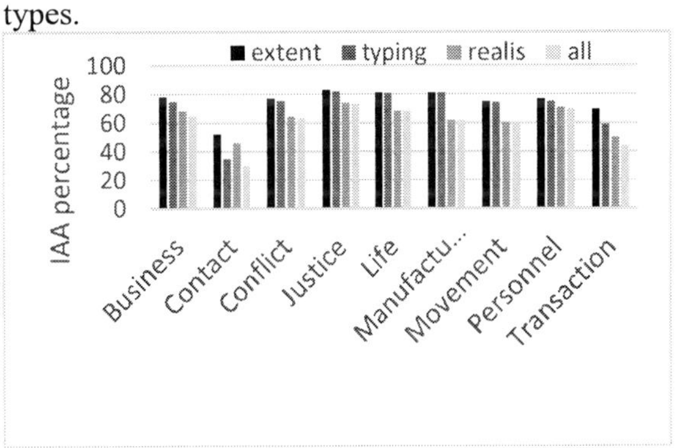

Figure 2: Inter-annotator agreement on first pass EN annotation 2015 by event types

5.2 Taggability

The annotation consistency can be attributed not only to disagreement in terms of event trigger, classification of event type and subtypes, realis attributes, but also misses and false alarms. Determining whether or not an event is taggable (i.e., recall) has always been a difficult issue in event annotation tasks, and some event types and subtypes still appear to be more heavily affected than others. To better understand the issue, we calculated the level of disagreement for event taggability by dividing the difference of event type-subtype counts in FP1 and FP2 by the event type-subtype count produced in the adjudication pass. Seventeen type-subtypes vary between FP1 and FP2 at a percentage below 10%, including Life.Divorce and Conflict.Attack, with some type-subtypes showing a high level of disagreement. As indicated in Figure 3, there are 12 type-subtypes with 20% or higher disagreement between FP1 and FP2, four of which are over 50%.

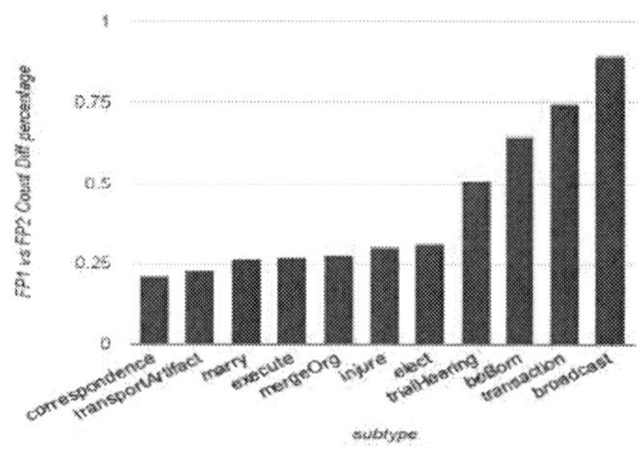

Figure 3: Difference of Event Nugget Occurrence between FP1 and FP2 over Adjudicated Occurrence.

Below are a few examples indicating disagreement in terms of taggability:

Miss:

- where she ***created*** (Business.StartOrg) the Davis Museum and Cultural Center.

False Alarm:

- She also ***owned*** (Transaction.TransferOwnership) a home in Northeast Harbor, Maine

5.3 Contact Event Type

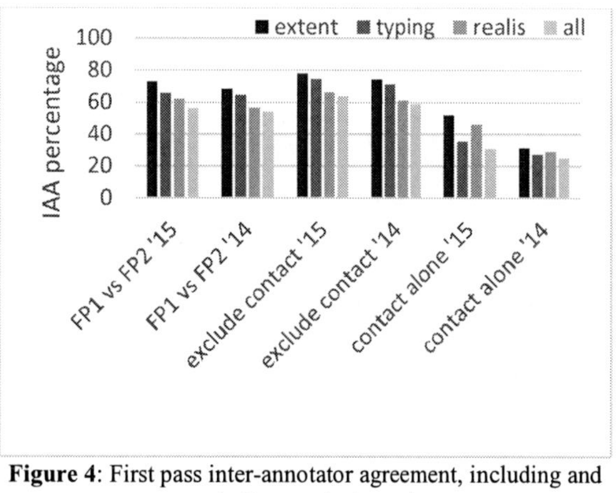

Figure 4: First pass inter-annotator agreement, including and excluding contact events.

One main change that we made in 2015 was the annotation of contact events, aiming to support a wider range of potential subtypes and also to improve annotation consistency. The subtypes were automatically determined based on the annotation of attributes in contact events, rather than by having annotators make a direct decision about contact subtypes.

There are 1479 event nuggets annotated with the contact type, which is 23% of all event nuggets in the evaluation data set. Contact.Broadcast and Contact.Contact are two of the most common subtypes. The consistency of the Contact event type annotation still poses challenges. As indicated in Figure 4, overall annotator consistency in both 2014 and 2015 improve when excluding the contact type from the comparison.

The consistency of contact events alone is much lower as compared with the other event types. This could be attributed to the taggability question of certain verbs. We have specified in the annotation guidelines that speech verbs such as "said" and "told" are taggable event triggers. We also specified that when there were multiple speech verbs instantiating the same contact event, only the first one is taggable. However, annotators vary in implementing this rule, as shown in the following example:

- *A spokesman for the Investigative Committee, a branch of the prosecutor's office, **said** (FP1: Contact.Broadcast) in an **interview** (FP2: Contact.Broadcast) in Izvestia.*

One positive thing we can see is that the changes in 2015 did improve the annotation consistency for contact events in 2015, but there is still room for further improvement, especially in the consistency of subtype classification of the Contact event type.

5.4 Double Tagging

Double tagging is quite common in the EN evaluation data set, due to the high frequency of Conflict.Attack/Life.Die, Transaction.TransferMoney and Transaction.TransferOwnership events. Altogether, 575 pairs out of 6440 event nuggets were double tagged (18%). Most of the double tagging cases are the result of the same trigger instantiating different event type-subtypes. Only 12 pairs of double tagging cases are the result of event argument conjunction. Figure 5 shows the distribution of event subtype counts involved in double tagging.

Double tagging was added to address the issue of inconsistency in event type categorization for triggers that may instantiate two or more event types and subtypes. Further analysis is needed to show whether allowing double tagging improves annotation consistency.

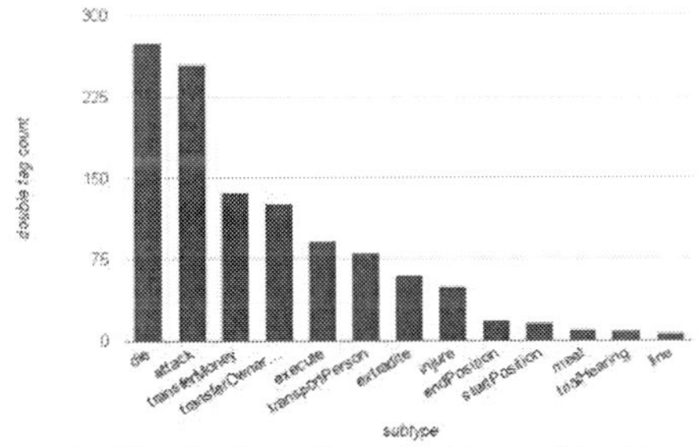

Figure 5: Distribution of event subtype of double tagging.

6 Annotation Challenges

One big challenge that annotators face is how to handle inferred events. Even though the annotation guidelines specifically instruct annotators not to tag any inferred events, whether an event mention is inferred not only depends on interpretation of the context, but also the meaning of the event triggers. Coupled with double tagging, this becomes a bigger issue. For example, in "*He then* ***trafficked*** *a large quatity of cocaine to the US.*", "trafficked" as defined as "buy or sell something illegally" is a trigger of Transaction.TransferOwnership event, but with the context of "to the US", it also indicates that the cocaine as been transported to the US. So it can also be a trigger for Movement.TransportArtifact event. One can argue that the Movement.TransportArtifact event is inferred, but it is still elusive to draw the boundary of inference.

As mentioned above, Contact event type poses a lot of difficulty and inference is one of the factors that contributes to this difficulty. The guidelines specify that regular speech verbs such as "say", "tell", and "speak" would be triggers for contact event types, but don't specify the other categories of reporting verbs, such as "argue", "advise", "order", or "testify", which involve more complicated interpretation. Some reporting verbs have not only the speech aspects, but also performative aspects, e.g., "testify", and "threaten". The question of whether to double tag such verbs (one for the contact type and one for the performative action) requires further discussion and clarification.

7 Conclusion and Future Work

In this paper, we described the annotation and evaluation of event nuggets and coreference in the TAC KBP evaluation. Annotated data has been distributed to DEFT and TAC KBP performers, and will be made available to the wider community as part of the Linguistic Data Consortium (LDC) catalog.

By analyzing the inter-annotator agreement between the two independent first pass annotations, we learned that some event types and subtypes are more difficult for annotators than others with respect to recall. We also learned that annotation consistency for event triggers has improved with the adoption of a minimal extent rule for event triggers in 2015 as compared with the maximal semantic extent unit rule in 2014's EN annotation, but inference is still a big challenge. Additionally, the contact event type still poses considerable difficulty. The addition of contact event attributes improved annotation consistency in 2015 as compared with that of 2014, but there is still room for improvement.

The detection and coreference of event nuggets provides an anchor for detecting event arguments and event-event relations. EN evaluation in TAC KBP 2015 attracted participation from 17 institutions, and NIST will continue to run an open evaluation of EN as part of the event track in TAC KBP 2016. The EN evaluation tasks will expand from English to multilingual, including Chinese and Spanish. Due to the scarcity of training data for some event types and subtypes, the set of event types and subtypes for the evaluation in 2016 will be reduced from 33 in 2014 evaluation and 38 in 2015 evaluation to 18 event types and subtypes.

Acknowledgments

This material is based on research sponsored by Air Force Research Laboratory and Defense Advanced Research Projects Agency under agreement number FA8750-13-2-0045. The U.S. Government is authorized to reproduce and distribute reprints for Governmental purposes notwithstanding any copyright notation thereon. The views and conclusions contained herein are those of the authors and should not be interpreted as necessarily representing the official policies or endorsements, either expressed or implied, of Air Force Research Laboratory and Defense Advanced Research Projects Agency or the U.S. Government.

References

Jacqueline Aguilar, Charley Beller, Paul McNamee, Benjamin Van Durme, Stephanie Strassel, Zhiyi Song, Joe Ellis. 2014. A Comparison of the Events and Relations Across ACE, ERE, TAC-KBP, and FrameNet Annotation Standards. ACL 2014: 52nd Annual Meeting of the Association for Computational Linguistics, Baltimore, June 22-27. *2nd Workshop on Events: Definition, Detection, Coreference, and Representation.*

Olga Babko-Malaya, Greg P. Milette, Michael K. Schneider, Sarah Scogin: Identifying Nuggets of Information in GALE Distillation Evaluation. In *Proceedings of the Fourth International Conference on Language Resources and Evaluation* (LREC 2012), Istanbul, May 21-27.

DARPA. 2012. Broad Agency Announcement: Deep Exploration and Filtering of Text (DEFT). Defense Advanced Research Projects Agency, DARPA-BAA-12-47.

George Doddington, Alexis Mitchell, Mark Przbocki, Lance Ramshaw, Stephanie Strassel, and Ralph Weischedel. 2004. The Automatic Content Extraction (ACE) program – tasks, data, and evaluation. In *Proceedings of the Fourth International Conference on Language Resources and Evaluation* (LREC 2004), Lisbon, May 24-30.

Joe Ellis, Jeremy Getman, Dana Fore, Neil Kuster, Zhiyi Song, Ann Bies, Stephanie Strassel. 2015. Overview of Linguistic Resources for the TAC KBP 2015 Evaluations: Methodologies and Results. In *Proceedings of TAC KBP 2015 Workshop, National Institute of Standards and Technology*, Gaithersburg, Maryland, USA, November 16-17, 2015.

Marjorie Freedman. 2015. TAC: Event Argument and Linking Evaluation task Description. http://www.nist.gov/tac/2015/KBP/Event/Argument/guidlines/EventArgumentAndLinkingTaskDescription.v09.pdf

Marjorie Freedman and Ryan Gabbard. 2014. Overview of the Event Argument Evaluation. In *Proceedings of TAC KBP 2014 Workshop, National Institute of Standards and Technology*, Gaithersburg, Maryland, USA, November 17-18, 2014.

Linguistic Data Consortium. 2005. ACE (Automatic-Content Extraction) English Annotation Guidelines for Events Version 5.4.3.

Zhengzhong Liu, Teruko Mitamura, Eduard Hovy. 2015. Evaluation Algorithms for Event Nugget Detection: A pilot Study. *3rd Workshop on EVENTS: Definition, Detection, Coreference, and Representation*, at the 2015 Conference of the North American Chapter of the Association for Computational Linguistics - Human Language Technologies (NAACL HLT 2015).

Teruko Mitamura, Eduard Hovy. 2015. TAC KBP Event Detection and Coreference Tasks for English. http://cairo.lti.cs.cmu.edu/kbp/2015/event/Event_Mention_Detection_and_Coreference-2015-v1.1.pdf.

Teruko Mitamura, Yukari Yamakawa, Sue Holm, Zhiyi Song, Ann Bies, Seth Kulick, Stephanie Strassel. 2015. Event Nugget Annotation: Processes and Issues. *3rd Workshop on EVENTS: Definition, Detection, Coreference, and Representation*, at the 2015 Conference of the North American Chapter of the Association for Computational Linguistics - Human Language Technologies (NAACL HLT 2015).

Ani Nenkova and Rebecca Passonneau. 2004. Evaluating content selection in summarization: the pyramid method. In Proceedings of the Human Language Technology Conference – North American chapter of the Association for Computational Linguistics annual meeting (NAACL-HLT 2004).

Ani Nenkova, Rebecca Passonneau, and Kathleen McKeown. 2007. The pyramid method: Incorporating human content selection variation in summarization evaluation. ACM Trans. Speech Lang. Process., 4(2):4.

Zhiyi Song, Ann Bies, Tom Riese, Justin Mott, Jonathan Wright, Seth Kulick, Neville Ryant, Stephanie Strassel, Xiaoyi Ma. 2015. From Light to Rich ERE: Annotation of Entities, Relations, and Events. *3rd Workshop on EVENTS: Definition, Detection, Coreference, and Representation*, at the 2015 Conference of the North American Chapter of the Association for Computational Linguistics - Human Language Technologies (NAACL HLT 2015).

Appendix

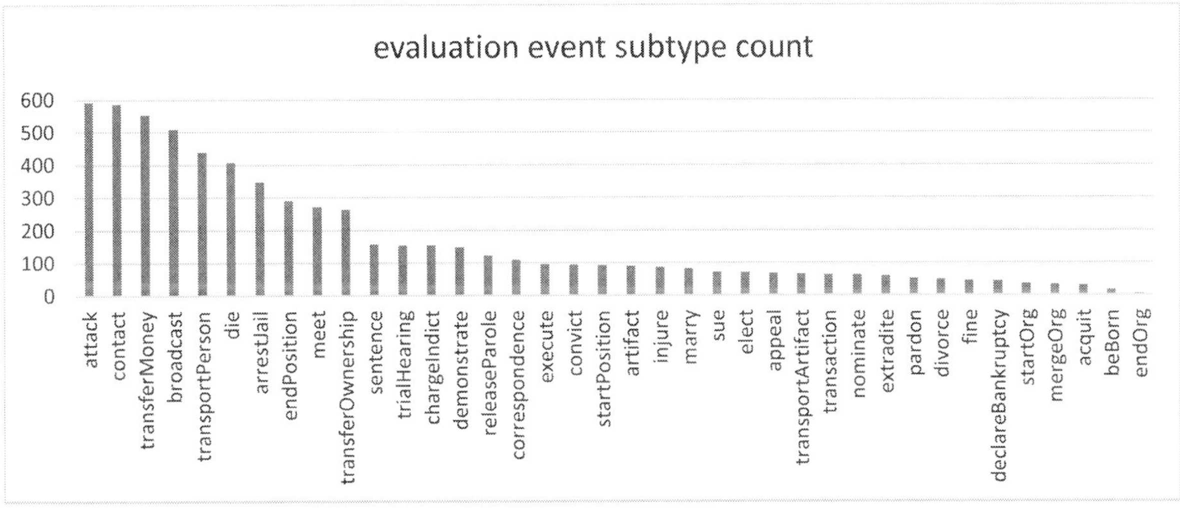

Event subtype distribution in Event Nugget 2015 Evaluation data

Constructing a Dictionary Describing Feature Changes of Arguments in Event Sentences

Tetsuaki Nakamura †
tnakamura@nlp.ist.i.kyoto-u.ac.jp

Daisuke Kawahara †‡
dk@i.kyoto-u.ac.jp

† Graduate School of Informatics,
Kyoto University

‡ JST PRESTO

Abstract

Common sense knowledge plays an essential role for natural language understanding, human-machine communication and so forth. In this paper, we acquire knowledge of events as common sense knowledge because there is a possibility that dictionaries of such knowledge are useful for recognition of implication relations in texts, inference of human activities and their planning, and so on. As for event knowledge, we focus on feature changes of arguments (hereafter, FCAs) in event sentences as knowledge of events. To construct a dictionary of FCAs, we propose a framework for acquiring such knowledge based on both of the automatic approach and the collective intelligence approach to exploit merits of both approaches. We acquired FCAs in event sentences through crowdsourcing and conducted the subjective evaluation to validate whether the FCAs are adequately acquired. As a result of the evaluation, it was shown that we were able to reasonably well capture FCAs in event sentences.

1 Introduction

Common sense knowledge plays an essential role for natural language understanding, human-machine communication and so forth. There are two approaches to acquire such knowledge. One is the automatic acquisition approach, the other is the manual acquisition approach. The automatic acquisition approach uses machine learning techniques and pattern matching methods. This approach is useful when the amount of data to be acquired is extremely large. However, the quality of acquired knowledge might be of low quality. The manual acquisition approach may use a fully manual technique (at very early stage of artificial intelligence studies) or collective intelligence (e.g., crowdsourcing and games with a purpose). This approach is useful for gathering subjective information, such as emotion information, which is difficult to acquire automatically.

In this paper, we acquire knowledge of events as common sense knowledge because there is a possibility that dictionaries of such knowledge are useful for recognition of implication relations in texts, inference of human activities and their planning, and so on. As for event knowledge, we focus on feature changes of arguments (hereafter, FCAs) in event sentences as knowledge of events because there are several studies of infant cognitive development (Massey and Gelman, 1988; Baillargeon et al., 1989; Spelke et al., 1995) that report that even infants use information about the basic features of participants in events to understand the events. There are some trials suggesting the possibility that dictionaries of FCAs are useful resources for deep understanding of texts (Rahman and Ng, 2012; Goyal et al., 2013). In (Rahman and Ng, 2012), features of relationships between event causalities and polarities (positive / negative) of participants in the events are used as features for anaphora resolution. In (Goyal et al., 2013), a dictionary of various binary effects (success(+/-), motivation(+/-), and so on) on characters caused by events (that is, verbs) are used for automatic story generation.

To construct a dictionary of FCAs, we propose a framework for acquiring such knowledge based on

Proceedings of the 4th Workshop on Events: Definition, Detection, Coreference, and Representation, pages 46–50,
San Diego, California, June 17, 2016.

both an automatic approach and a manual approach (collective intelligence) that exploits merits of both approaches. That is, we acquire seed knowledge by using collective intelligence and expand the knowledge automatically.

2 Related Work

Many studies have aimed at automatically acquiring relationships between events (Chambers and Jurafsky, 2009; Chambers and Jurafsky, 2010; Vanderwende, 2005; Shibata et al., 2014). However, these studies do not focus on the motivation of events or effects caused by the events. Although we can determine which events occur after an event by using the dictionaries constructed in such studies, we cannot understand why the events occur. For example, although we may know the event "a girl cries" happens after another event "a girl gets injured" by using the dictionary, we cannot understand why the former event occurs. To understand the motivation of the former event, we have to know that "the girl feels pain." Of course, the problem can be solved by treating the phenomenon "the girl feels pain" as an event and describing it in the dictionary. However, such a policy requires infinite descriptions. It is preferable to form and maintain the dictionary with an controlled granularity.

In the case that participants in events are animated beings, events may influence their emotions. Many studies developing software to process human emotions exploits models proposed by psychologists (Hasegawa et al., 2013; Tokuhisa et al., 2008; Tokuhisa et al., 2009; Vu et al., 2014). In these studies, Ekman's Big Six Model (Ekman, 1992) and Plutchik's wheel of emotions (Plutchik, 1980) are used to automatically extract emotion knowledge from large corpora. However, since these studies do not focus on what happens after evoking various changes of emotions, they are not able to understand complex phenomenon involving such changes.

Some dictionaries constructed manually that retain high quality are available. For example, ConceptNet[1] built in the Open Mind Common Sense project (Singh, 2002) and a large-scale knowledge database built in the CYC project (Lenat, 1995) are available. The database built in the VerbCorner project (Hartshorne et al., 2014), expanding of VerbNet (Kipper et al., 2000) through crowdsourcing, is also available. However, these studies do not focus on the granularity of knowledge.

For the controlled granularity, we focus on the use of basic level features of arguments in event sentences. Since both of animate beings and inanimate objects can be arguments in sentences, we assume not only physical features but also mental features. The decision criteria for these features are described in Section 3.2.

[1] http://conceptnet5.media.mit.edu/

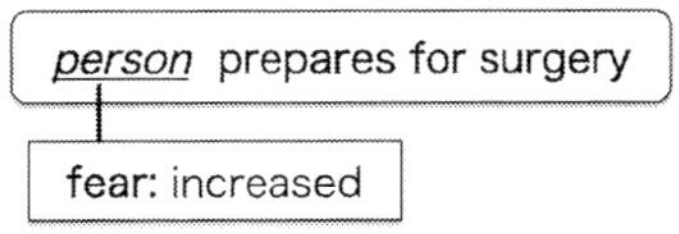

Figure 1: Example entry in the proposed dictionary. Event sentences are associated with FCAs.

3 Proposal

3.1 Architecture

To construct a knowledge database that keeps an controlled granularity and can be used to understand the motivation of events, we focus on the feature changes of arguments (FCAs) in event sentences. Our purpose is to construct a dictionary that has the architecture shown in Figure 1. As shown in the figure, the dictionary describes relationships between events and FCAs in the event sentences.

3.2 Features

As described in Section 2, we focus on the use of basic level features of arguments in event sentences. We assume 16 features listed in Table 1 to be associated with arguments in event sentences. As for physical basic level features, we regard eight features listed in the Table as basic level features because we pay attention to the traditional sense categories ("sight", "hearing", "smell", "taste", and "touch"). As for mental basic level features, we use basic emotions (e.g., eight mental features listed in the Table) of Plutchik's model (Plutchik, 1980) because the model assumes other emotions derived from the basic emotions systematically.

Category	Features	Degrees
physical	form, color, touch, smell, sound, taste, location, temperature	changed, unchanged, irrelevant
mental	joy, fear, trust, surprise, anger, disgust, sadness, expectation	increased, decreased, unchanged, irrelevant

Table 1: Features of arguments.

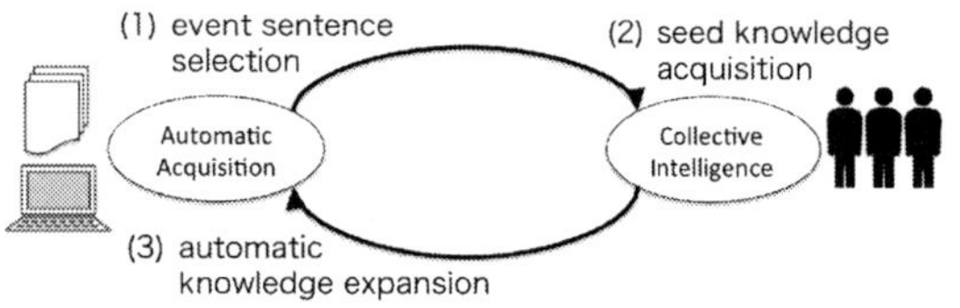

Figure 2: Expansion of our dictionary. We used automatic procedures and crowdsourcing to expand the size of the dictionary.

3.3 Construction Method

We are planning to construct the dictionary described in section 3.1 based on both of automatic procedure and collective intelligence as follows: (PHASE 1) Frequent event sentences are selected automatically. (PHASE 2) FCAs of the selected sentences are acquired as seed knowledge based on crowdsourcing because our dictionary is designed to deal with subjective information such as emotions. (PHASE 3) Knowledge is automatically expanded by using the seed knowledge.

The sequence of precedures described above is illustrated in Figure 2. We intend to expand the size of our dictionary based on the loop.

4 Experiment

We conducted an experiment to validate whether FCAs in event sentences are adequately acquired by using crowdsourcing.

4.1 Data

We created event sentences presented to crowdsourcing workers based on the "Kyoto University Web Document Leads Corpus (KWDLC) (Hangyo et al., 2012)"[2] and the "Kyoto University Case Frames (KUCF) (Kawahara and Kurohashi, 2006)."[3] The KWDLC is a Japanese text corpus that comprises 5,000 documents (15,000 sentences) with annotations of morphology, named entities, dependencies, predicate-argument structures including zero anaphora and coreferences. The KUCF is a database of case frames automatically constructed from 1.6 billion Japanese sentences taken from Web pages. The KUCF has about 40,000 predicates, with 13 case frames on average for each predicate.

The sentence creation procedure is as follows. (STEP 1) The 200 most frequent verbs were extracted from the KWDLC. (STEP 2) Verbs that are very abstract (e.g., "do") were omitted. As a result, 167 verbs remained. (STEP 3) The top two frequent arguments were used as the representative arguments of each case frame (meaning) of each verb. (STEP 4) Sentences were created by combining the verbs with their representative arguments. As a result, 1,935 Japanese sentences were created. (STEP 5) Sentences that were difficult to understand were pruned based on crowdsourcing[4]. The crowdsourcing workers were asked to answer whether they could understand the presented sentences. Each sentence was judged by 10 workers. In total, 244 people participated in the task. For each sentence, we estimated the probability that the "yes" was selected by using the method proposed in (Whitehill et al., 2009) and omitted sentences with probabilities less than 0.9. As a result, 857 event sentences remained and 148 verbs (types) were included in the sentences. Since each of these sentences had two or three arguments, 1,768 arguments (token) were obtained as a result.

4.2 Method

FCAs in event sentences were acquired through a crowdsourcing task. In the task, workers were asked to answer questions about feature changes of arguments in the presented event sentences as shown in Figure 3. Every worker was given a set which includes an event sentence and five questions about FCAs in the sentence. The argument was randomly selected from the 1,768 arguments described above. Although five features to be asked were selected from the 16 features in Table 1 for each task, FCAs of all the features for each argument were acquired in total. 2,910 people (token) were participated in this experiment. The each worker could be engaged in a maximum of five tasks and each feature was judged by 10 workers.

[2] http://nlp.ist.i.kyoto-u.ac.jp/EN/index.php?DDLC

[3] http://www.gsk.or.jp/en/catalog/gsk2008-b/

[4] http://crowdsourcing.yahoo.co.jp/

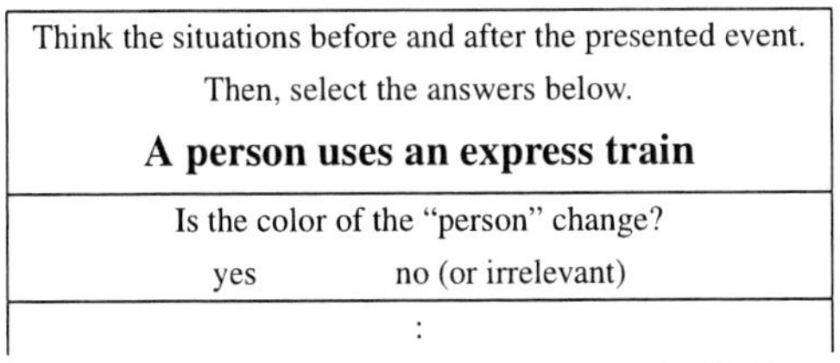

Figure 3: Layout examples of the task to acquire FCAs (physical features). Each task is composed of an event sentence and five questions about FCAs in the sentence. In the case of mental features, four options (increased, decreased, unchanged, and irrelevant) are used.

We used the method proposed by Whitehill et al. (2009) to estimate the probability of each option for each feature. These probabilities are estimated jointly incorporating the difficulty of each question and the answering skill of each worker according to the agreements of the collected judges. Therefore, the estimated probabilities are more reliable than the results of a simple counting method such as majority voting. The probabilities were used as elements in vectors expressing the FCAs (hereafter, FCA vectors). Moreover, we assigned ten workers to each question to better ensure reliability, since it is reported that annotation results provided by more than six non-expert workers are close to those provided by expert labelers (Snow et al., 2008).

4.3 Results

For example, in the case of "a child" as in "a child gets a fever," the estimated probabilities that the labels "increased" of "temperature" and "fear" were selected were 0.99. To validate whether FCAs in event sentences were adequately acquired by using crowdsourcing, we conducted a subjective evaluation as follows: (STEP 1) Ten arguments with salient elements of FCA vectors were selected (hereafter, query arguments: QAs) from 1,768 arguments. (STEP 2) For each QA, a list of arguments with impressions similar to the QA was obtained (candidate arguments: CAs). The lists were composed of the five most similar arguments. In this paper, "arguments with similar impressions" means arguments which have similar FCA vectors. We used cosine similarities between FCA vectors as similarities. (STEP 3) For each list, five judges (people engaged in studies of natural language processing) were asked to answer whether each CA was similar to the corresponding QA (similar = 2 points, a little similar = 1 point, different = 0 point).

As a result, the average point of CAs was 1.24. (For QAs with salient physical FCAs, the average point was 1.08. For QAs with salient mental FCAs, the average point was 1.40) This result suggests that FCAs were adequately acquired through crowdsourcing. Especially, it was shown that the result of QAs with salient mental FCAs was better than that of QAs with salient physical FCAs. We speculate that the reason was due to the granularities of values (that is, "whether features are changed (three options: changed, unchanged, irrelevant)" v.s. "how features are changed (four options: increased, decreased, unchanged, irrelevant)").

5 Conclusion

In this paper, we focused on feature changes of arguments (FCAs) in event sentences as knowledge of events and acquire the FCAs as common sense knowledge through crowdsourcing. As a result of the subjective evaluation to validate whether the FCAs are adequately acquired by using crowdsourcing, it was shown that we were able to reasonably well capture the FCAs.

In the next step, we must consider the automatic method that expand the size of our dictionary by using seed knowledge as described in Section 3.3. For the expansion, we are planning to analyze knowledge acquired in this study because we anticipate that there are FCAs to be shared and those not to be shared. That is, we think that there are three types of FCAs at least: (1) FCAs mainly depend on verbs themselves (e.g., disgust that "girl" feels in "A boy complains to a girl"), (2) FCAs mainly depend on combinations of arguments and verbs (e.g., color of "water" in "He pour his orange juice into the water"), and (3) FCAs mainly depend on contexts (e.g., joy that "girl" feels in "A girl see a boy"; the girl's emotion depends on whether she likes him).

For the future work, we are also planning to construct a large scale network in which structures described in Figure 1 are regarded as units and the units associated with related units are linked each other.

Note that the patent for the architecture described in this paper is pending at the time of writing this paper.

References

Renee Baillargeon, Julia Devos, and Marcia Graber. 1989. Location memory in 8-month-old infants in a non-search ab task: Further evidence. *Cognitive Development*, 4(4):345–367.

Nathanael Chambers and Dan Jurafsky. 2009. Unsupervised learning of narrative schemas and their participants. In *the Joint Conference of the 47th Annual Meeting of the ACL and the 4th International Joint Conference on Natural Language Processing of the AFNLP*, pages 602 –610.

Nathanael Chambers and Dan Jurafsky. 2010. A database of narrative schemas. In *the Seventh International Conference on Language Resources and Evaluation (LREC2010)*.

Paul Ekman. 1992. An argument for basic emotions. *Cognition and Emotion*, 6:169–200.

Amit Goyal, Ellen Riloff, and Hal Daumé III. 2013. A computational model for plot units. *Computational Intelligence*, 29(3):466–488.

Masatsugu Hangyo, Daisuke Kawahara, and Sadao Kurohashi. 2012. Building a diverse document leads corpus annotated with semantic relations. In *the 26th Pacific Asia Conference on Language Information and Computing*, pages 535–544.

Joshua K. Hartshorne, Claire Bonial, and Martha Palmer. 2014. The verbcorner project: Findings from phase 1 of crowd-sourcing a semantic decomposition of verbs. In *the 52nd Annual Meeting of the Association for Computational Linguistics*, pages 397–402.

Takayuki Hasegawa, Nobuhiro Kaji, Naoki Yoshinaga, and Masashi Toyoda. 2013. Predicting and eliciting addressee's emotion in online dialogue. In *the 51st Annual Meeting of the Association for Computational Linguistics*, pages 964–972.

Daisuke Kawahara and Sadao Kurohashi. 2006. Case frame compilation from the web using high-performance computing. In *the 5th International Conference on Language Resources and Evaluation (LREC2006)*, pages 1344–1347.

Karin Kipper, Hoa Trang Dang, and Martha Palmer. 2000. Class-based construction of a verb lexicon. In *the 7th National Conference of Artificial Intelligence*, pages 691–696.

Douglas B. Lenat. 1995. Cyc: a large-scale investment in knowledge infrastructure. *Commun. ACM*, 38(11):33–38.

Christine M. Massey and Rochel Gelman. 1988. Preschoolers' ability to decide whether a photographed unfamiliar object can move itself. *Developmental Psychology*, pages 307–317.

Robert Plutchik, 1980. *A General Psychoevolutionary Theory of Emotion, 1*, pages 3–33. Academic Press.

Altaf Rahman and Vincent Ng. 2012. Resolving complex cases of definite pronouns: The winograd schema challenge. In *Proceedings of the 2012 Joint Conference on Empirical Methods in Natural Language Processing and Computational Natural Language Learning*, pages 777–789.

Tomohide Shibata, Shotaro Kohama, and Sadao Kurohashi. 2014. A large scale database of strongly-related events in japanese. In *the 9th International Conference on Language Resources and Evaluation (LREC2014)*, pages 3283–3288.

Push Singh. 2002. The open mind common sense project.

Rion Snow, Brendan O'Connor, Daniel Jurafsky, and Andrew Y. Ng. 2008. Cheap and fast – but is it good? evaluating non-expert annotations for natural language tasks. In *Proceedings of the 2008 Conference on Empirical Methods in Natural Language Processing*, pages 254–263.

Elizabeth S. Spelke, Ann Phillips, and Amanda L. Woodward, 1995. *Infants' knowledge of object motion and human action*. Oxford University Press.

Ryoko Tokuhisa, Kentaro Inui, and Yuji Matsumoto. 2008. Emotion classification using massive examples extracted from the web. In *the 22nd International Conference on Computational Linguistics*, pages 881–888.

Ryoko Tokuhisa, Kentaro Inui, and Yuji Matsumoto. 2009. Emotion classification using massive examples extracted from the web. *Journal of Information Processing (in Japanese)*, 50(4):1365–1374.

Lucy Vanderwende. 2005. Volunteers created the web. In *Proceedings of the 2005 AAAI Spring Symposium, Knowledge Collection from Volunteer Contributors*.

Hoa Trong Vu, Graham Neubig, Sakriani Sakti, Tomoki Toda, and Satoshi Nakamura. 2014. Acquiring a dictionary of emotion-provoking events. In *the 14th Conference of the European Chapter of the Association for Computational Linguistics*, pages 128–132.

Jacob Whitehill, Paul L. Ruvolo, Jacob Bergsma Ting-fan Wu, and Javier R. Movellan, 2009. *Whose Vote Should Count More: Optimal Integration of Labels from Labelers of Unknown Expertise*, volume 22, pages 2035–2043. Curran Associates, Inc.

CaTeRS: Causal and Temporal Relation Scheme for Semantic Annotation of Event Structures

Nasrin Mostafazadeh[1], **Alyson Grealish**[1], **Nathanael Chambers**[2], **James Allen**[1,4], **Lucy Vanderwende**[3]

1 University of Rochester, 2 United States Naval Academy,
3 Microsoft Research, 4 The Institute for Human & Machine Cognition

{nasrinm, agrealis, james}@cs.rochester.edu
nchamber@usna.edu, lucyv@microsoft.com

Abstract

Learning commonsense causal and temporal relation between events is one of the major steps towards deeper language understanding. This is even more crucial for understanding stories and script learning. A prerequisite for learning scripts is a semantic framework which enables capturing rich event structures. In this paper we introduce a novel semantic annotation framework, called Causal and Temporal Relation Scheme (CaTeRS), which is unique in simultaneously capturing a comprehensive set of temporal and causal relations between events. By annotating a total of 1,600 sentences in the context of 320 five-sentence short stories sampled from ROCStories corpus, we demonstrate that these stories are indeed full of causal and temporal relations. Furthermore, we show that the CaTeRS annotation scheme enables high inter-annotator agreement for broad-coverage event entity annotation and moderate agreement on semantic link annotation.

1 Introduction

Understanding events and their relations in natural language has become increasingly important for various NLP tasks. Most notably, story understanding (Charniak, 1972; Winograd, 1972; Turner, 1994; Schubert and Hwang, 2000) which is an extremely challenging task in natural language understanding, is highly dependent on understanding events and their relations. Recently, we have witnessed a renewed interest in story and narrative understanding based on the progress made in core NLP tasks.

Perhaps the biggest challenge of story understanding (and story generation) is having commonsense knowledge for the interpretation of narrative events. This commonsense knowledge can be best represented as scripts. Scripts present structured knowledge about stereotypical event sequences together with their participants. A well known script is the Restaurant Script, which includes the events {Entering, Sitting down, Asking for menus, Choosing meals, etc.}, and the participants {Customer, Waiter, Chef, Tables, etc.}. A large body of work in story understanding has focused on learning scripts (Schank and Abelson, 1977). Given that developing hand-built scripts is extremely time-consuming, there is a serious need for automatically induced scripts (Chambers and Jurafsky, 2008; Chambers and Jurafsky, 2009; Balasubramanian et al., 2013; Cheung et al., 2013; Nguyen et al., 2015). It is evident that various NLU applications (text summarization, co-reference resolution and question answering, among others) can benefit from the rich inferential capabilities that structured knowledge about events can provide.

The first step for any script learner is to decide on a corpus to drive the learning process. The most recent resource for this purpose is a corpus of short commonsense stories, called ROCStories (Mostafazadeh et al., 2016), which is a corpus of 40,000 short commonsense everyday stories [1]. This corpus contains high quality[2] five-sentence stories

[1] These stories can be found here: http://cs.rochester.edu/nlp/rocstories

[2] Each of these stories have the following major characteristics: is realistic, has a clear beginning and ending where something happens in between, does not include anything irrelevant

Proceedings of the 4th Workshop on Events: Definition, Detection, Coreference, and Representation, pages 51–61,
San Diego, California, June 17, 2016.

that are full of stereotypical causal and temporal relations between events, making them a perfect resource for learning narrative schemas.

One of the prerequisites for learning scripts from these stories is to extract events and find inter-event semantic relations. Earlier work (Chambers and Jurafsky, 2008; Chambers and Jurafsky, 2009; Pichotta and Mooney, 2014; Rudinger et al., 2015) defines verbs as events and uses TimeML-based (Pustejovsky et al., 2003) learning for temporal ordering of events. This clearly has many shortcomings, including, but not limited to (1) not capturing a wide range of non-verbal events such as 'earthquake', (2) not capturing a more comprehensive set of semantic relations between events such as causality, which is a core relation in stories.

In this paper we formally define a new comprehensive semantic framework for capturing stereotypical event-event temporal and causal relations in commonsense stories, the details of which can be found in Sections 2-4. Using this semantic framework we annotated 320 stories sampled from ROCStories to extract inter-event semantic structures. Our inter-annotator agreement analysis, presented in Section 5 shows that this framework enables high event entity annotation agreement and promising inter-event relation annotation agreement. We believe that our semantic framework better suits the goals of the task of script learning and story understanding, which can potentially enable learning richer and more accurate scripts. Although this work focuses on stories, the CaTeRS annotation framework for capturing inter-event relations can be applied to other genres.

2 Event Entities

Our semantic framework captures the set of event entities and their pairwise semantic relations, which together form an inter-connected network of events. In this Section we define event entities and discuss their annotation process.

2.1 Definition

Event is mainly used as a term referring to any situation that can happen, occur, or hold. The definition and detection of events has been a topic of interest in various NLP applications. However, there is still no consensus regarding the span of events and how they should be annotated. There has been some good progress in domain-specific annotation of events, e.g., recent Clinical TempEval task (Bethard, 2013) and THYME annotation scheme (Styler et al., 2014), however, the detection of events in broad-coverage natural language has been an ongoing endeavor in the field.

One of the existing definitions for event is provided in the TimeML annotation schema (Pustejovsky et al., 2003):

> "An event is any situation (including a process or state) that happens, occurs, or holds to be true or false during some time point (punctual) or time interval (durative)."

According to this definition, adjectival states such as 'on board' are also annotated as events. As we are focused on the task of narrative structure learning, we want to capture anything that 'happens and occurs', but not including holds. Formally, we therefore define an event as follows:

> "An event is any situation (including a process or state) that happens or occurs either instantaneously (punctual) or during a period of time (durative)."

In order to make the event annotation less subjective, we specifically define an event to be any lexical entry under any of the following ontology types in the TRIPS ontology[3] (Allen et al., 2008):

- Event-of-state: e.g., have, lack.
- Event-of-change: e.g., kill, delay, eat.
- Event-type: e.g., effort, procedure, turmoil, mess, fire.
- Physical-condition: all medical disorders and conditions, e.g., cancer, heart attack, stroke, etc.
- Occurring: e.g., happen, occur.
- Natural-phenomenon: e.g., earthquake, tsunami.

This ontology has one of the richest event hierarchies, which perfectly serves our purpose of broad-coverage event extraction.

2.2 How to annotate events?

After pinpointing an event entity according to the formal definition presented earlier, one should annotate the event by selecting the corresponding span

to the core story.

[3] http://www.cs.rochester.edu/research/trips/lexicon/browse-ont-lex-ajax.html

in the sentence. Here, we define the event span to be the head of the main phrase which includes the complete event. For example, in the sentence 'I [climbed] the tree', we annotate 'climb', the head of the verb phrase, while the complete event is '[climb] tree' . This implies that only main events (and not their dependents) are annotated. Annotating the head word enables us to delegate the decision about adding the dependent children to a post-process, which can be tuned per application.

Moreover, no verbs which take the role of an auxiliary verb are annotated as events. For instance, in the sentence 'She had to [change] her jeans' the main event is 'change'. For multi-word verbs such as 'turn out or 'find out', the entire span should be selected as the event. The annotators can consult lexicons such as WordNet (Miller., 1995) for distinguishing multi-word verbs from verbs with prepositional phrases adjuncts.

2.2.1 The Case for Embedded Events

Another important controversial issue is what to do with embedded events, where one event takes another event as its core argument (if neither of the verbs are auxiliary). For instance, consider the following example:

(1) Sam [wanted]$_{e1}$ to [avoid]$_{e2}$ any trouble, so he [drove]$_{e3}$ slowly.

According to our event entity definition, there are three events in example 1, $e1$ and $e2$ and $e3$, all of which should be annotated. However, more complicated is the case of a main event in an embedded event construction which signals any of the semantic relations in the annotation scheme. Consider the sentence in example 2. In this sentence, there are also three events according to our definition of event entities, where (cause (die)) is an embedded event construction. In this case the verb 'cause' simply signals a causal relation between $e1$ and $e3$, which will be captured by our existing semantic relation (to be described in Section 3), and so we do not annotate the verb 'cause' as an event.

Likewise, the sentence in example 3 showcases another embedded event construction, (cause (explosion)), so the event 'cause' should not be annotated.

(2) The [explosion]$_{e1}$ caused him to [die]$_{e3}$.

(3) The [fire]$_{e1}$ caused an [explosion]$_{e2}$.

The same rule applies to the synonyms of these verbs in addition to other verbs that signal a temporal or causal relation, including but not limited to {start, begin, end, prevent, stop, trigger}, which hereinafter we call 'aspectual verbs'[4]. It is important to note that the above rule for aspectual verbs can be applied only to embedded event constructions and may be overridden. Consider example 4. In this example, it is clear that the event 'prevent' plays a key semantic role in the sentence and should be annotated as an event since it is the only viable event that can be semantically connected to other events such as $e3$.

(4) John [prevented]$_{e1}$ the vase from [falling]$_{e2}$ off the table, I was [relieved]$_{e3}$.

2.3 The Case for Copulas

A copula is a verb which links the subject of a sentence with a predicate, such as the verb 'is' which links 'this suit' to the predicate 'dark blue' in the sentence 'This suit is dark blue'. Many such constructions assign a state to something or someone which holds true for some duration. The question is what to specify as the event entity in such sentences. According to our definitions, an adjective such as 'blue' is not an event (that is, it does not occur or happen), but after many rounds of pilot annotations, we concluded that annotating the predicate adjective or predicate nominal best captures the core semantic information. Thus, the sentences 5-6 will be annotated as follows:

(5) He was really [hungry]$_{e1}$.

(6) He [ate]$_{e1}$ a juicy burger.

It is important to emphasize that annotating states such as 'hungry' as an event is only done in the case of copulas, and, for example in sentence 6, the adjective 'juicy' will not be annotated as an event.

Our annotation of light verb constructions (e.g., do, make, have) is consistent with the annotation of copulas and auxiliary verbs. Whenever the semantic contribution of the verb is minimal and the non-verb element of the construction is an event in the

[4]These verbs are the same as aspectual events characterized by TimeML, which include 'INITIATES', 'CULMINATES', 'TERMINATES', 'CONTINUES' and 'REINITIATES'.

TRIPS ontology, we annotate the non-verb element as the event. Thus, we annotate the noun predicate 'offer' in the sentence 'Yesterday, John made an offer to buy the house for 350,000', similarly to the way Abstract Meaning Representation (AMR) drops the light verb and promotes the noun predicate (Banarescu et al., 2013). This annotation is also close to the PropBank annotation of copulas and light verbs (Bonial et al., 2014), where they annotate the noun predicate and predicate adjective as the event; however, PropBank includes an explicit marking of the verb as either a light verb or a copula verb.

3 The Semantic Relations Between Event Entities

A more challenging problem than event entity detection is the identification of the semantic relation that holds between events. Events take place in time, hence temporal relations between events are crucial to study. Furthermore, causality plays a crucial role in establishing semantic relation between events, specifically in stories. In this Section, we provide details on both temporal and causal semantic relations.

3.1 Temporal Relation

Time is the main notion for anchoring the changes of the world triggered by sequences of events. Of course having temporal understanding and temporal reasoning capabilities is crucial for many NLP applications such as question answering, text summarization and many others. Throughout the years the issue of temporal analysis and reasoning in natural language has been addressed via different approaches. Allen's Interval Algebra (Allen, 1984) is one theory for representing actions and introduces a set of 13 distinct, exhaustive, and qualitative temporal relations that can hold between two time intervals. The first three columns of Table 1 list these 13 temporal relations together with their visualization, which includes 6 main relations and their corresponding inverses –together with the 'equal' relation which does not have an inverse.

Based on Interval Algebra, a new markup language for annotating events and temporal expressions in natural language was proposed (Pustejovsky et al., 2003), named TimeML. This schema is designed to address problems in event and temporal expression markup. It covers two major tags: 'EVENT' and 'TIMEX3'. The EVENT tag is used to annotate elements in a text that represent events such as 'kill' and 'crash'. TIMEX is mainly used to annotate explicit temporal expressions, such as times, dates and durations. One of the major features introduced in TimeML was the LINK tag. These tags encode the semantic relations that exist between the temporal elements annotated in a document. The most notable LINK is TLINK: a Temporal Link representing the temporal relationship between entities (events and time expressions). This link not only encodes a relation between two entities, but also makes a partial ordering between events. There are 14 TLINK relations in TimeML, adding 'simultaneous' to the list of temporal links between events. The fourth column of Table 1 shows the correspondence between Allen relations and TimeML TLINKs. Furthermore, in the fifth column we include the THYME annotation schema (to be discussed in Section 6).

We propose a new set of temporal relations for capturing event-event relations. Our final set of temporal relations are shown in the sixth column of Table 1[5]. As compared with TimeML, we drop the relations 'simultaneous', 'begins' and 'ends'. 'Simultaneous' was not a part of the original Allen relations. Generally it is hard to be certain about two events occurring exactly during the same time span, starting together and ending together. Indeed, the majority of events which are presumed 'simultaneous' in TimeML annotated corpora are either (1) EVENT-TIMEX relations which are not event-event relations, or (2) wrongly annotated and should be the 'overlapping' relation, e.g., in the following sentence from TimeBank corpus the correct relation for the two events $e1$ and $e2$ should be 'overlap':

She [listened]$_{e1}$ to music while [driving]$_{e2}$.

We acknowledge that having 'simultaneous' can make the annotation framework more comprehensive and may apply in few certain cases of punctual events, however, such cases are very rare in our corpus, and in the interest of a more compact and less ambiguous annotation, we did not include

[5]Since a main temporal relation and its inverse have a reflexive relation, the annotation is carried out only on the main temporal relation.

Allen	Visualization	Allen - Inverse	TimeML	THYME	CaTeRS
X Before Y		Y After X	Before	Before	Before
X Meets Y		Y Is Met X	IBefore (Immediately)	-	-
X Overlaps Y	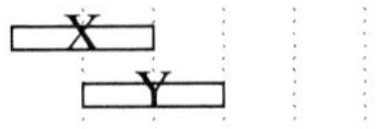	Y Is overlapped by X	-	Overlaps	Overlaps
X Finishes Y	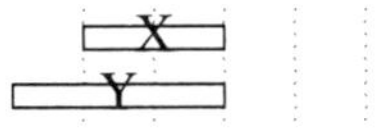	Y Is finished by X	Ends	Ends-on	-
X Starts Y	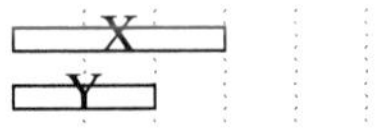	Y Is started by X	Begins	Begins-on	-
X Contain Y	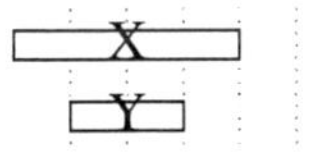	Y During X	During	Contains	Contains
X Equals Y		-	Identity	Identity	Identity
-	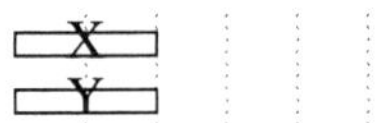	-	Simultaneous	-	-

Table 1: The correspondence of temporal relation sets of different annotation frameworks.

it. THYME also dropped 'simultaneous' for similar reasons.

As for the 'begins' and 'ends', our multiple pilot studies, indicated that these relations are more accurately captured by one of our causal relations (next subsection) or the relation 'overlaps'. We believe that our simplified set of 4 temporal relations can be used for any future broad-coverage inter-event temporal relation annotation. We also drop the temporal relation 'IBefore', given that this relation usually reflects on causal relation between two events which will be captured by our causal links.

3.2 Causal Relation

Research on the extraction of event relations has concerned mainly the temporal relation and time-wise ordering of events. A more complex semantic relationship between events is causality. Causality is one of the main semantic relationships between events where an event (CAUSE) results in another event (EFFECT) to happen or hold. It is clear that identifying the causal relation between events is crucial for numerous applications, including story understanding. Predicting occurrence of future events is the major benefit of causal analysis, which can itself help risk analysis and disaster decision making. There is an obvious connection between causal relation and temporal relation: by definition, the CAUSE event starts 'BEFORE' the EFFECT event. Hence, predicting causality between two events also requires/results in a temporal prediction.

It is challenging to define causality in natural language. Causation, as commonly understood as a notion for understanding the world in the philosophy and psychology, is not fully predicated in natural language (Neeleman and Koot, 2012). There have been several attempts in the field of psychology for modeling causality, e.g., the counterfactual model (Lewis, 1973) and the probabilistic contrast model (Cheng and Novick, 1992). Leonard Talmy's seminal work (Talmy, 1988) in the field of cognitive linguistics models the world in terms of semantic categories of how entities interact with respect to force (Force Dynamics). These semantic categories include concepts such as the employment of force, resistance to force and the overcoming of resistance, blockage of a force, removal of blockage, and etc. Force dynamics provides a generalization over the traditional linguistic understanding of causation by categorizing causation into 'letting', 'helping', 'hindering' and etc. Wolff and Song (Wolff and Song, 2003) base their theory of causal verbs on force dynamics. Wolff proposes (Wolff, 2007) that causation includes three main types of *causal concepts*: **'Cause', 'Enable'** and **'Prevent'**. These three causal concepts are lexicalized through distinctive types of verbs (Wolff and Song, 2003) which are as follows:

– Cause-type verbs: e.g. cause, start, prompt, force.

– Enable-type verbs: e.g. allow, permit, enable, help.

– Prevent-type verbs: e.g. block, prevent, hinder, restrain.

Wolff's model accounts for various ways that causal concepts are lexicalized in language and we base our annotation framework on this model. However, we will be looking at causal relation between events more from a **'commonsense reasoning'** perspective than linguistic markers. We define cause, enable and prevent for commonsense co-occurrence of events, inspired by mental model theory of causality (Khemlani et al., 2014), as follows:

– A $Cause$ B: In the context, If A occurs, B most probably occurs as a result.

– A $Enable$ B: In the context, If A does not occur, B most probably does not occur (not enabled to occur).

– A $Prevent$ B: In the context, If A occurs, B most probably does not occur as a result.

where *In the context* refers to the underlying context in which A and B occur, such as a story. This definition is in line with the definition of CAUSE and PRECONDITION presented in the RED annotation guidelines (Ikuta et al., 2014) (to be discussed in Section 6).

In order to better understand the notion of commonsense causality, consider the sentences 7-9.

(7) Harry [fell]$_{e1}$ and [skinned]$_{e2}$ his knee.

(8) Karla [earned]$_{e1}$ more money and finally [bought]$_{e2}$ a house.

(9) It was [raining]$_{e1}$ so hard that it prevented me from [going]$_{e2}$[6] to the school.

[6]As discussed earlier, here the embedded event construction is (prevent (going)) where only the event 'going' will be annotated.

In the above three sentences, the relation between $e1$ and $e2$ is 'cause', 'enable' and 'prevent' in order.

It is important to note that our scope of lexical semantic causality only captures events causing events (Davidson, 1967), however, capturing individuals as cause (Croft, 1991) is a another possible extension.

3.2.1 Temporal Implications of Causality

The definition of causality implies that when A Causes B, then A should start before B in order to have triggered it. It is important to note that for durative events the temporal implication of causality is mainly about the start of the causal event, which should be before the start of the event which is caused. Consider the following example:

(10) The [fire]$_{e1}$ [burned down]$_{e2}$ the house.

In this example there is a 'cause' relation between $e1$ and $e2$, where 'fire' clearly does not finish before starting of the 'burn' event. So the temporal relation between the two events is 'overlaps'. Here we conclude that when 'A cause/enable/prevent B', we know as a fact that As start is before Bs start, but there is no restriction on their relative ending. This implies that a cause relation can have any of the two temporal relations: *before* and *overlaps*.

All the earlier examples of causal concepts we explored involved an event causing another event to happen or to start (in case of a durative event). However, there are examples of causality which involve not starting but ending an ongoing event. Consider the sentence 11. In order to capture causality relations between pairs of events such as $e1$ and $e2$, we introduce a *Cause-to-end* relation, which can have one of the three temporal implications: *before*, *overlaps*, and *during*. Hence, in sentence 11, the relation between $e1$ and $e2$ will be *Cause-to-end (overlap)*.

(11) The [famine]$_{e1}$ ended the [war]$_{e2}$.

3.3 How to annotate semantic relations between events?

In summary, the disjunctive[7] set of 13 semantic relations between events in our annotation framework are as follows:

[7]This implies that only one of these semantic relations can be selected per each event pair.

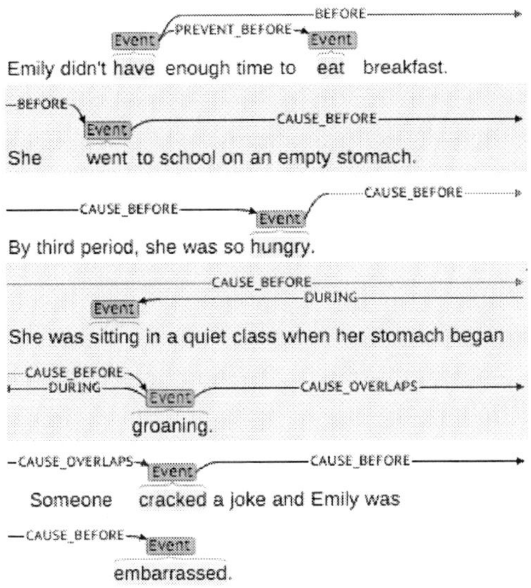

Figure 1: Semantic annotation of a sample story.

– **9 causal relations:** Including 'cause (before/overlaps)', 'enable (before/overlaps)', 'prevent (before/overlaps)', 'cause-to-end (before/overlaps/during)'

– **4 temporal relations:** Including 'Before', 'Overlaps', 'Contains', 'Identity'.

The semantic relation annotation between two events should start with deciding about any causal relations and then, if there was not any causal relation, proceed to choosing any existing temporal relation.

4 Annotating at Story level

It has been shown (Bittar et al., 2012) that temporal annotation can be most properly carried out by taking into account the full context for sentences, as opposed to TimeML, which is a surface-based annotation. The scope and goal of this paper very well aligns with this observation. We carry out the annotation at the story level, meaning that we annotate inter-event relations across the five sentences of a story. It suffices to do the event-event relation specification minimally given the transitivity of temporal relations. For example for three consecutive events $e1$ $e2$ $e3$ one should only annotate the 'before' relation between $e1$ and $e2$, and $e2$ and $e3$, since the 'before' relation between $e1$ and $e3$ can be inferred from the other two relations. The event-event relations can be from/to any sentence in the story. It is important to emphasize here that the goal of annotation is to capture commonsensical relations between events, so the annotation effort should be driven by intuitive commonsensical relation one can pinpoint throughout a story.

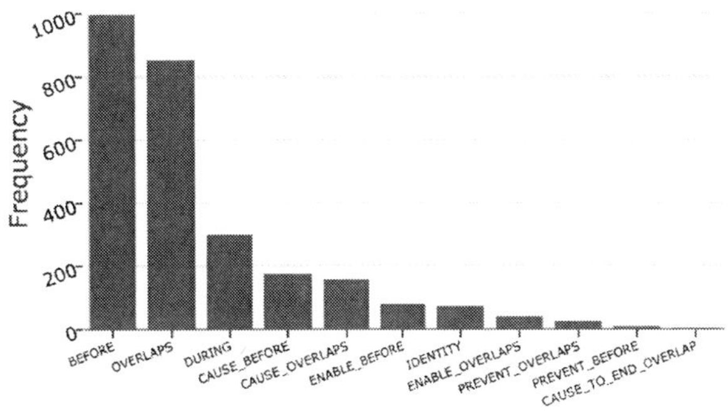

Figure 2: Frequency of semantic links in our dataset.

Consider an example of a fully annotated story shown in Figure 1. As you can see, all of the semantic annotations reflect commonsense relation between events given the underlying story, e.g., 'cracked a joke' *cause-before* 'embarrassed'.

5 Annotated Dataset Analysis

We randomly sampled 320 stories (1,600 sentences) from the ROCStories Corpus. This set covers a variety of everyday stories, with titles ranging from 'got a new phone' to 'Left at the altar'. We provided our main expert annotator with the annotation guidelines, with the task of annotating each of the 320 stories at story level. The annotation task was set up on Brat tool[8]. On average, annotation time per story was 11 minutes. These annotations can be found through `http://cs.rochester.edu/nlp/rocstories/CaTeRS/`.

5.1 Statistics

Overall, we have annotated 2,708 event entities and 2,715 semantic relations. Figure 2 depicts the distribution of different semantic relations in our annotation set. For this Figure we have removed any semantic relations with frequency less than 5. As you can see, the temporal relation *before* is the most common relation, which reflects on the natural reporting of the sequence of events throughout a

[8] `http://brat.nlplab.org/`

story. There are overall 488 various causal links, the most frequent of which is *cause-before*. Given these statistics, it is clear that capturing causality along with temporal aspects of stories is crucial.

Our annotations also enable some deeper analysis of the narrative flow of the stories. One major question is if the text order of events appearing in consecutive sentences mirrors the real-world order of events. Although the real-world order of events is more complex than just a sequence of *before* relations, we can simplify our set of semantic links to make an approximation: we count the number of links (from any[9] type) which connect an event entity appearing in position X to an event entity appearing in position $X - i$. We found that temporal order does not match the text order 23% of the time. This reinforces the quality of the narrative flow in the ROCStories corpus. Moreover, 23% is statistically significant enough to motivate the requirement for temporal ordering models for these stories.

5.2 Inter-annotator Agreement

In order to compute inter-annotator agreement on our annotation framework, we shared one batch of 20 stories between four expert annotators. Our annotation task consists of two subtasks: (1) entity span selection: choosing non-overlapping event entity spans for each story, (2) semantic structure annotation: building a directed graph (most commonly connected) on top of the entity spans.

5.2.1 Agreement on Event Entities

Given that there are no prefixed set of event entity spans for straight-forward computation of inter-annotator agreement, we do the following: among all the annotators, we aggregate the spans of the annotated event entity as the annotation object (Artstein and Poesio, 2008). Then, if there exists a span which is not annotated by one of the coders (annotators) it will be labeled as 'NONE' for its category. The agreement according to Fleiss's Kappa $\kappa = 0.91$, which shows substantial agreement on event entity annotation. Although direct comparison of κ values is not possible, as a point of reference, the event span annotation of the most recent clinical TempEval (Bethard et al., 2015) was 0.81.

5.2.2 Agreement on Semantic Links

Decisions on semantic links are dependent on two things (1) decisions on event entities; (2) the decision about the other links. Hence, the task of annotating event structures is in general a hard task. In order to relax the dependency on event entities, we fix the set of entities to be the ones that all annotators have agreed on. Following the other discourse structure annotation tasks such as Rhetorical Structure Theory (RST), we aggregate all the relations captured by all annotators as the annotation object, then labeling 'NONE' as the category for coders who have not captured this relation. The agreement according to Fleiss's Kappa $\kappa = 0.49$ without applying basic closure and $\kappa = 0.51$ with closure[10], which shows moderate agreement. For reference, the agreement on semantic link annotation in the most recent clinical TempEval was 0.44 without closure and 0.47 with closure.

6 Related Work

One of the most recent temporal annotation schemas is Temporal Histories of Your Medical Event (THYME) (Styler et al., 2014). This annotation guideline was devised for the purpose of establishing timelines in clinical narratives, i.e. the free text portions contained in electronic health records. In their work, they combine the TimeML annotation schema with Allen Interval Algebra, identifying the five temporal relations BEFORE, OVERLAP, BEGINS-ON, ENDS-ON, and CONTAINS. Of note is that they adopt the notion of narrative containers (Pustejovsky and Stubbs, 2011), which are time slices in which events can take place, such as DOCTIME (time of the report) and before DOCTIME. As such, the THYME guideline focuses on ordering events with respect to specific time intervals, while in our work, we are only focused on the relation between two events, without concern for ordering. Their simplification of temporal links is similar to ours, however, our reasoning for simplification takes

[9]This is based on the fact that any relation such as 'A enable-before B' or 'A overlaps B' can be naively approximated to 'A before B'.

[10]Temporal closure (Gerevini et al., 1995) is a reasoning for deriving explicit relations to implicit relations, applying rules such as transitivity.

into account the existence of causality, which is not captured by THYME.

Causality is a notion that has been widely studied in psychology, philosophy, and logic. However, precise modeling and representation of causality in NLP applications is still an open issue. A formal definition of causality in lexical semantics can be found in (Hobbs, 2005). Hobbs introduces the notion of "causal complex", which refers to some collection of eventualities (events or states) for which holding or happening entails the happening of effect. In part, our annotation work is motivated to learn what the causal complexes are for a given event or state. The Penn Discourse Tree Bank (PDTB) corpus (Prasad et al., 2008) addresses the annotation of causal relations, annotating semantic relations that hold between exactly two Abstract Objects (called Arg1 and Arg2), expressed either explicitly via lexical items or implicitly via adjacency in discourse. In this paper, we present a semantic framework that captures both explicit and implicit causality, but no constraint of adjacency is imposed, allowing commonsense causality to be captured at the inter-sentential level (story).

Another line of work annotates temporal and causal relations in parallel (Steven Bethard and Martin, 2008). Bethard et al. annotated a dataset of 1,000 conjoined-event temporal-causal relations, collected from Wall Street Journal corpus. Each event pair was annotated manually with both temporal (BEFORE, AFTER, NO-REL) and causal relations (CAUSE, NO-REL). For example, sentence 12 is an entry in their dataset. This dataset makes no distinction between various types of causal relation.

(12) Fuel tanks had leaked and contaminated the soil.
- (leaked BEFORE contaminated)
- (leaked CAUSED contaminated).

A recent work (Mirza and Tonelli, 2014) has proposed a TimeML-style annotation standard for capturing causal relations between events. They mainly introduce 'CLINK', analogous to 'TLINK' in TimeML, to be added to the existing TimeML link tags. Under this framework, Mirza et al (Mirza and Tonelli, 2014) annotates 318 CLINKs in TempEval-3 TimeBank. They only annotate explicit causal relations signaled by linguistic markers, such as {because of, as a result of, due to, so, therefore, thus}. Another relevant work is Richer Event Descriptions (RED) (Ikuta et al., 2014), which combines event coreference and THYME annotations, and also introduces cause-effect annotation in adjacent sentences to achieve a richer semantic representation of events and their relations. RED also distinguishes between 'PRECONDITION' and 'CAUSE', similarly to our 'ENABLE' and 'CAUSE' relations. These can be in the context of BEFORE or OVERLAP, but they do not include PREVENT and CAUSE-TO-END. Our set of comprehensive 9 causal relations distinguishes between various temporal implications, not covered by any of the related work.

7 Conclusion

In this paper we introduced a novel framework for semantic annotation of event-event relations in commonsense stories, called CaTeRS. We annotated 1,600 sentences throughout 320 short stories sampled from ROCStories corpus, capturing 2,708 event entities and 2,715 semantic relations, including 13 various types of causal and temporal relations. This annotation scheme is unique in capturing both temporal and causal inter-event relations. We show that our annotation scheme enables high inter-annotator agreement for event entity annotation. This is due to our clear definition of events which (1) is linked to lexical entries in TRIPS ontology, removing problems caused by each annotator devising his or her own notion of event, (2) captures only the head of the underlying phrase.

Our inter-annotator analysis of semantic link annotation shows moderate agreement, competitive with earlier temporal annotation schemas. We are planning to improve the agreement on semantic links even further by setting up two-stage expert annotation process, where we can pair annotators for resolving disagreements and modifying the annotation guideline. A comprehensive study of temporal and causal closure in our framework is a future work.

We believe that our semantic framework for temporal and causal annotation of stories can better model the event structures required for script and narrative structure learning. Although this work focuses on stories, our annotation framework for capturing inter-event relations can be applicable to other genres. It is important to note that this framework is not intended to be a comprehensive analysis of all temporal and causal aspects of text, but rather we focus on those temporal and causal links that support learning stereotypical narrative structures. As with any annotation framework, this framework will keep evolving over time, the updates of which can be followed through `http://cs.rochester.edu/nlp/rocstories/CaTeRS/`.

Acknowledgments

We thank Martha Palmer and the anonymous reviewers for their invaluable and extensive comments on this paper. This work was supported in part by Grant W911NF-15-1-0542 with the US Defense Advanced Research Projects Agency (DARPA), the Army Research Office (ARO) and Office of Naval Research (ONR).

References

James F. Allen, Mary Swift, and Will de Beaumont. 2008. Deep semantic analysis of text. In *Proceedings of the 2008 Conference on Semantics in Text Processing*, STEP '08, pages 343–354, Stroudsburg, PA, USA. Association for Computational Linguistics.

James F. Allen. 1984. Towards a general theory of action and time. *Artif. Intell.*, 23(2):123–154, July.

Ron Artstein and Massimo Poesio. 2008. Inter-coder agreement for computational linguistics. *Comput. Linguist.*, 34(4):555–596, December.

Niranjan Balasubramanian, Stephen Soderland, Oren Etzioni Mausam, and Oren Etzioni. 2013. Generating coherent event schemas at scale. In *EMNLP*, pages 1721–1731.

Laura Banarescu, Claire Bonial, Shu Cai, Madalina Georgescu, Kira Griffitt, Ulf Hermjakob, Kevin Knight, Philipp Koehn, Martha Palmer, and Nathan Schneider. 2013. Abstract meaning representation for sembanking.

Steven Bethard, Leon Derczynski, Guergana Savova, James Pustejovsky, and Marc Verhagen. 2015. Semeval-2015 task 6: Clinical tempeval. In *Proceedings of the 9th International Workshop on Semantic Evaluation (SemEval 2015)*, pages 806–814, Denver, Colorado, June. Association for Computational Linguistics.

Steven Bethard. 2013. Cleartk-timeml: A minimalist approach to tempeval 2013. In *Second Joint Conference on Lexical and Computational Semantics (*SEM), Volume 2: Proceedings of the Seventh International Workshop on Semantic Evaluation (SemEval 2013)*, pages 10–14, Atlanta, Georgia, USA. Association for Computational Linguistics.

Andr Bittar, Caroline Hagge, Vronique Moriceau, Xavier Tannier, and Charles Teissdre. 2012. Temporal annotation: A proposal for guidelines and an experiment with inter-annotator agreement. In Nicoletta Calzolari (Conference Chair), Khalid Choukri, Thierry Declerck, Mehmet Uur Doan, Bente Maegaard, Joseph Mariani, Asuncion Moreno, Jan Odijk, and Stelios Piperidis, editors, *Proceedings of the Eight International Conference on Language Resources and Evaluation (LREC'12)*, Istanbul, Turkey, may. European Language Resources Association (ELRA).

Claire Bonial, Julia Bonn, Kathryn Conger, Jena D. Hwang, and Martha Palmer. 2014. Propbank: Semantics of new predicate types. In Nicoletta Calzolari (Conference Chair), Khalid Choukri, Thierry Declerck, Hrafn Loftsson, Bente Maegaard, Joseph Mariani, Asuncion Moreno, Jan Odijk, and Stelios Piperidis, editors, *Proceedings of the Ninth International Conference on Language Resources and Evaluation (LREC'14)*, Reykjavik, Iceland, may. European Language Resources Association (ELRA).

Nathanael Chambers and Daniel Jurafsky. 2008. Unsupervised learning of narrative event chains. In Kathleen McKeown, Johanna D. Moore, Simone Teufel, James Allan, and Sadaoki Furui, editors, *ACL*, pages 789–797. The Association for Computer Linguistics.

Nathanael Chambers and Dan Jurafsky. 2009. Unsupervised learning of narrative schemas and their participants. In *Proceedings of the Joint Conference of the 47th Annual Meeting of the ACL and the 4th International Joint Conference on Natural Language Processing of the AFNLP: Volume 2 - Volume 2*, ACL '09, pages 602–610, Stroudsburg, PA, USA. Association for Computational Linguistics.

Eugene Charniak. 1972. Toward a model of children's story comprehension. December.

Patricia W. Cheng and Laura R. Novick. 1992. Covariation in natural causal induction. *Psychological Review*, 99(2):365382.

Jackie Cheung, Hoifung Poon, and Lucy Vanderwende. 2013. Probabilistic frame induction. In *ACL*.

William. Croft. 1991. *Syntactic categories and grammatical relations : the cognitive organization of information / William Croft.* University of Chicago Press Chicago.

Donald Davidson. 1967. Causal relations. *Journal of Philosophy*, 64(21):691–703.

Alfonso Gerevini, Lenhart K. Schubert, and Stephanie Schaeffer. 1995. The temporal reasoning tools timegraph i-ii. *International Journal on Artificial Intelligence Tools*, 4(1-2):281–300.

Jerry R. Hobbs. 2005. Toward a useful concept of causality for lexical semantics. *Journal of Semantics*, 22(2):181–209.

Rei Ikuta, Will Styler, Mariah Hamang, Tim O'Gorman, and Martha Palmer. 2014. Challenges of adding causation to richer event descriptions. In *Proceedings of the Second Workshop on EVENTS: Definition, Detection, Coreference, and Representation*, pages 12–20, Baltimore, Maryland, USA, June. Association for Computational Linguistics.

Sangeet Khemlani, Aron K Barbey, and Philip Nicholas Johnson-Laird. 2014. Causal reasoning with mental models. *Frontiers in Human Neuroscience*, 8(849).

David Lewis. 1973. *Counterfactuals*. Blackwell Publishers, Oxford.

G. Miller. 1995. Wordnet: A lexical database for english. In *In Communications of the ACM*.

Paramita Mirza and Sara Tonelli. 2014. An analysis of causality between events and its relation to temporal information. In *COLING 2014, 25th International Conference on Computational Linguistics, Proceedings of the Conference: Technical Papers, August 23-29, 2014, Dublin, Ireland*, pages 2097–2106.

Nasrin Mostafazadeh, Nathanael Chambers, Xiaodong He, Devi Parikh, Dhruv Batra, Lucy Vanderwende, Pushmeet Kohli, and James Allen. 2016. A corpus and cloze evaluation for deeper understanding of commonsense stories. In *Proceedings of NAACL HLT*, San Diego, California, June. Association for Computational Linguistics.

Ad Neeleman and Hans Van De Koot. 2012. The theta system: Argument structure at the interface. *The Linguistic Expression of Causation*, pages 20–51.

Kiem-Hieu Nguyen, Xavier Tannier, Olivier Ferret, and Romaric Besançon. 2015. Generative event schema induction with entity disambiguation. In *Proceedings of the 53rd annual meeting of the Association for Computational Linguistics (ACL-15)*.

Karl Pichotta and Raymond J Mooney. 2014. Statistical script learning with multi-argument events. *EACL 2014*, page 220.

Rashmi Prasad, Nikhil Dinesh, Alan Lee, Eleni Miltsakaki, Livio Robaldo, Aravind K. Joshi, and Bonnie L. Webber. 2008. The penn discourse treebank 2.0. In *LREC*. European Language Resources Association.

James Pustejovsky and Amber Stubbs. 2011. Increasing informativeness in temporal annotation. In *Proceedings of the 5th Linguistic Annotation Workshop*, LAW V '11, pages 152–160, Stroudsburg, PA, USA. Association for Computational Linguistics.

James Pustejovsky, Jos Castao, Robert Ingria, Roser Saur, Robert Gaizauskas, Andrea Setzer, and Graham Katz. 2003. Timeml: Robust specification of event and temporal expressions in text. In *Fifth International Workshop on Computational Semantics (IWCS-5*.

Rachel Rudinger, Pushpendre Rastogi, Francis Ferraro, and Benjamin Van Durme. 2015. Script induction as language modeling. In *Proceedings of the 2015 Conference on Empirical Methods in Natural Language Processing (EMNLP-15)*.

Roger C. Schank and Robert P. Abelson. 1977. *Scripts, Plans, Goals and Understanding: an Inquiry into Human Knowledge Structures*. L. Erlbaum, Hillsdale, NJ.

Lenhart K. Schubert and Chung Hee Hwang. 2000. Episodic logic meets little red riding hood: A comprehensive, natural representation for language understanding. In *Natural Language Processing and Knowledge Representation: Language for Knowledge and Knowledge for Language*. MIT/AAAI Press.

Sara Klingenstein Steven Bethard, William Corvey and James H. Martin. 2008. Building a corpus of temporal-causal structure. In Bente Maegaard Joseph Mariani Jan Odijk Stelios Piperidis Daniel Tapias Nicoletta Calzolari (Conference Chair), Khalid Choukri, editor, *Proceedings of the Sixth International Conference on Language Resources and Evaluation (LREC'08)*, Marrakech, Morocco, may. European Language Resources Association (ELRA). http://www.lrec-conf.org/proceedings/lrec2008/.

IV William F. Styler, Steven Bethard, Sean Finan, Martha Palmer, Sameer Pradhan, Piet C. de Groen, Brad Erickson, Timothy Miller, Chen Lin, Guergana Savova, and James Pustejovsky. 2014. Temporal annotation in the clinical domain. *Transactions of the Association for Computational Linguistics*, 2:143–154.

Leonard Talmy. 1988. Force dynamics in language and cognition. *Cognitive Science*, 12(1):49–100.

Scott R. Turner. 1994. The creative process: A computer model of storytelling. *Hillsdale: Lawrence Erlbaum.*

Terry Winograd. 1972. *Understanding Natural Language*. Academic Press, Inc., Orlando, FL, USA.

Phillip Wolff and Grace Song. 2003. Models of causation and the semantics of causal verbs. *Cognitive Psychology*, 47(3):276–332.

Phillip Wolff. 2007. Representing causation. *Journal of Experiment Psychology: General*, 136:82111.

Association for Computational Linguistics
209 N. Eighth Street
Stroudsburg, Pennsylvania 18360

ISBN 978-1-5108-2520-8

CURRAN ASSOCIATES INC.
proceedings.com